JESUS THE SUFI
THE LOST DIMENSION OF CHRISTIANITY

Second Edition

T0163777

Max Gorman

AEON

First published in 2018 by
Aeon Books Ltd
118 Finchley Road
London NW3 5HT

British Library Cataloguing in Publication Data

A C.I.P. for this book is available from the British Library

ISBN-13: 978-1-91159-708-7

Typeset by Medlar Publishing Solutions Pvt Ltd, India

www.aeonbooks.co.uk

JESUS THE SUFI

The author, born in India, was educated in a convent
in the Himalayas, and also by a hermit
in the jungle near Delhi, before the influence of
mystic, rather than academic Oxford.

He is a poet with little sympathy for the 'poetry'
of his times—and a jazz pianist, particularly
influenced by George Shearing.

For those who wonder whether there might be something else, after all.

ACKNOWLEDGEMENTS

I wish to thank Mr Aubrey Wolton for the particular assistance he has given me in writing this book, Anna Sullivan for her constant encouragement throughout, Andrew Kean for his supportive interest in, and excellent typing of, the manuscript, and Paul Ferguson for his accurate scrutiny of the proof.

I owe much to my original publishers Greg Meanwell and Robin Campbell for their helpful suggestions with regard to the book, and for what I can only describe as their faith in its contents.

I am most grateful to Oliver Rathbone, of Aeon Books, for the publication of this second edition of the book, so that it can continue to reach those whom it is meant to reach. And for the kind and able assistance of Cecily Blench in this process.

I also wish to thank Octagon Press for their kind permission to quote from the works of Idries Shah, in particular 'The Sufi Quest' from *Thinkers of the East*, and the stories 'Strike on this Spot' and 'The King's Son' from *Tales of the Dervishes*.

The author and publishers acknowledge the following for rights to reproduce: The M.C. Escher Company for M.C. Escher's 'Three Worlds' © 2005 the M.C. Escher Company—Holland. All rights reserved. www.mcescher.com; Bruce Blankinship for the photograph of the Fatehpur Sikri inscription; the Bibliothèque

Nationale de France for the image of the Chain of Being; Paul Fricker for 'St. Francis in the Marshes'; Anne-Marie Sullivan for her illustration of Jesus' saying; the Estate of Eric Gill/ Bridgeman Art Library for 'Who Were the First to Cry Nowell'.

Author's note

When using the term 'man' I mean of course humanity in both its kinds.

The angels keep their ancient places—
Turn but a stone and start a wing!
'Tis ye, 'tis your estrangèd faces
That miss the many-splendoured thing.

Francis Thompson

In my Father's house are many mansions.

Jesus of Nazareth

Man lives only in the cellar of his house.

G. I. Gurdjieff

You think that what the wise have taught about extra dimensions for mankind is absurd. And yet you can conceive that a butterfly which lives only for a day may regard the concept of 'a week' as a ridiculous fantasy.

Idries Shah

CONTENTS

CONTENTS

PREFACE

I had always suspected as a child in India that there was more to Jesus than met either the eye of my father, in those days a fervent atheist who allowed he was 'a very excellent man', or that of his unlikely friend, the equally fervent Bishop of Bombay who, when he visited us, bombastically attempted to counter his influence with a view of Christianity that, even at the age of eleven, I found as dubious as it was doleful.

These were the last years of the Raj—which I survived by disappearing for long periods of the day into the jungle growing not far from our large white bungalow on the edge of Delhi. Wandering there one afternoon I came across an overgrown ruin in whose creeper-covered portal stood a semi-naked, bearded figure, who was to become a particular influence upon my childhood education.

I'd say he was about fifty years of age, though at the time I neither knew nor cared.

He summoned me in a voice I felt I could trust, and handed me a chapatti to dip into the earthenware bowl of delicious vegetable curry he placed between us. We soon became friends, and I would visit him regularly for a chat and a chapatti in what he told me was a ruined palace. This Indian gentleman—he never told me his name or asked me mine—shared this abode, I was to discover, with a monkey, a mongoose, and a large cobra.

Curiously the snake and the mongoose never showed the slightest inclination to fight. I now put this down to the presence of this unusual man.

Our talks ranged over many things. One day he asked me who I thought Jesus was. I said I didn't really know—but I liked the sound of him.

'And do you believe he did all those miracles?'

I paused for a while. 'I don't see why not.'

'Good,' he said quietly. 'And what about your parents?'

I explained my father's position. To my surprise he nodded acceptingly.

'My mother never mentions Jesus, but she believes in God.' He nodded again. Then I told him about the Bishop—and he laughed uproariously but benevolently.

'Jesus—the *only* son of God? What about *you*, my boy? You have it in you too. But you have to make it grow. Like that mustard seed he was always talking about. We can all be God's sons and daughters—if we work for it. As *he* did.'

Years later, when I had come to this other extraordinary country, England, my education in the Indian jungle, combined with the influence of Oxford—mystic rather than academic of course—helped me to recognise first Gurdjieff, and then the Sufis and their connection with Jesus. By Sufis I do not mean 'Islamic mystics'—the common misconception—but masters of an ancient tradition of inner teaching, free-moving, not bound by religion or culture, but directed at the essential human being.

Hujwiri, Suhrawardi and other eminent Sufis have supported this universal conception of the Way of the Sufi. They aver that it existed both before and beyond Islam. That it is neither of the East nor the West, but belongs and beckons to all mankind. As the Sufi authority and historian Idries Shah has more recently said: 'Sufism has been known under many names, to all peoples from the beginning of human times.' And, curiously, the apparently orthodox St. Augustine, in one of his rare moments of insight, wrote in one of his Letters: 'That which is called Christianity existed among the ancients, and never did not exist from the beginning of the human race.'[1]

That Jesus of Nazareth was a Sufi master is clear from his distinctive use of stories for teaching purposes, his sayings, and his what Sufis call 'action-teachings' including those unusual actions known as miracles, which they regard as instruments of inner development.

I find that Sufism illuminates from within concepts central to Christianity: baptism, resurrection, Son of God, the Kingdom of Heaven—which can then be seen as states and stages in the development of human consciousness. They spring into organic life. The Sufi searchlight, like an ultraviolet beam shone onto the petals of flowers, reveals hidden meanings and messages, normally invisible.

Max Gorman, 2017

Note

1. *Epistolae Liber I.xii, page 3.*

INTRODUCTION

Who are the Sufis? And why should we call Jesus one? These are the questions this book seeks to answer. In doing so, a view of the man and his teaching will emerge which differs as much from the orthodox Christian's image of him as 'the one and only son of God', as it does from the equally common opinion that he was simply a great and good 'ordinary' man.

Sufis have always regarded Jesus of Nazareth as their kind of man, and a master of their Way. So naturally many of his parables and sayings have been in constant use by them as teaching material, together with the work of other teachers of their Tradition. They maintain, however, that the inner potential of such material can only be released in the context of a true Sufi school, under the direction of a teaching master. This is a *sine qua non* of the enterprise. And for this and other reasons the movement known today as 'Christianity' has long lost sight of the real nature and original purpose of these teachings. It is submitted that to regard Jesus as primarily a teacher of ethics is to miss the point. Focus on the ethical dimension of his message, important as it undoubtedly is, has occluded perception of its evolutionary dimension.

Nowhere is this more clearly illustrated than in the misunderstanding of the Greek term *metanoia* which has been wrongly translated as 'repentance' in the Gospels, but which in fact means 'change or transformation of consciousness', from *meta*—change, towards 'beyondness'—and *noia*—consciousness—from *nous*, the faculty of inner perception.

Jesus, then, and his colleague John the Baptist, were not exhorting us to indulge in an orgy of remorse of conscience, but challenging us to engage in an adventure of consciousness.

Paul, despite an opacity in several other respects, does seem to have understood this. 'Be not conformed to this world: but be ye transformed by the renewing of your *nous*'. (Romans 12.2). And so did the early Christian mystic St. Anthony, who tells us: 'The soul sees by means of the nous ... but it is blind unless the *nous* is purified'. (*The Philokalia*: Volume 1)

A. K. Coomaraswamy was the first to draw attention to the seriousness of the obfuscation being discussed, in his essay 'On Being in One's Right Mind' (1941): 'It is indeed unfortunate that our word 'repentance' translates *metameleia* rather than *metanoia*; for the latter word imports far more than the merely moral meaning of regret for past errors. Metanoia is a transformation of one's whole being; from human thinking to divine understanding.'

Maurice Nicoll arrived at the same idea independently, and developed it further in his book *The Mark* (1954). 'The real meaning of human life is not to be found in external life, but in the idea of a transformation which, happening within a man, leads to a state called the "Kingdom of Heaven" ... It is this new idea, this change, that is indicated by the word *metanoia*, which is so poorly and so inadequately translated as "repentance." '

Finally, the poet and Christian esotericist Robin Amis, having described metanoia as a 'change in the gravity of the intelligence'—that is intelligence in the fullest, deepest sense—puts the whole thing beautifully: 'The nous is the knowing power of the inmost heart, known as the eye of the soul: and metanoia, the change of nous, is a change of heart.' (*A Different Christianity*, 1995)

It becomes possible then in the light of the foregoing to re-phrase 'Unless ye repent, ye cannot enter the Kingdom of Heaven' as: 'Unless you change your consciousness you cannot enter the Kingdom of Heaven.'

If one can accept that a certain higher level or quality of knowledge depends on a parallel higher level of being and consciousness, one can see Jesus is describing this transformation in another way in this little-known saying of his recorded by the great philosopher and Sufi, Al Ghazali (known as Algazel in the West): 'Jesus, son of Mary, (Peace be upon him!) has said: "Verily I say unto you, he who has not been born twice will not see the kingdom of the heavens and the earth. The first birth is the birth of nature, and the second birth is the birth of the spirit in the heaven of knowledge."'

One cannot but be reminded of his words at John 3.3: 'Verily, verily I say unto thee, except a man be born again he cannot enter the kingdom of God.' Followed by: 'Except a man be born of water, and the spirit, he cannot enter into the kingdom of God. That which is born of the flesh is flesh; and that which is born of the spirit is spirit.'

Obviously two variations on the same theme, each valuably complementing the other.

And the message, which the Sufis share with Jesus and certain other colleagues—is clear: Man has possibilities of development he knows not of. With rightly guided effort he can realise these possibilities. He is at present only half awake, living only in the 'ante-room' of his life.

Which is why Jesus said: 'I am come that they might have life, and have it more abundantly.'[1] (John 10.10)

Note

1. The Greek word *perissos* has the connotation 'superior'— implying a qualitative rather than a quantitative change.

CHAPTER ONE

The way of the Sufi

The way of the Sufi is the way *to* the Sufi. By which is meant that the object of Sufism is to produce Sufis. A Sufi is a 'Complete Man'[1], which implies that a man or a woman as usually found, in the 'normal' state, is incomplete. When Jesus said: 'Be ye perfect as your Father in Heaven is perfect,' (Matthew 5.48) he was exhorting his disciples to realise their potential completeness as human beings, their full development, and become as perfectly human, as God was perfectly God.

Sufis have always recognised Jesus himself as a 'complete man' of this kind, for only a complete man can assist others to attain this state. This must be obvious. Only someone who has already travelled the Way is able to guide others along it. And such guidance is essential.

As Sirajudin Abbasi, Sufi and scholar, wrote of the Sufis in his seventeenth century work *Safarnama*:

> If you revere them as saints, you will benefit from their sainthood; but if you work with them as associates, you will benefit from their company. To them the world is a fashioning instrument, which polishes mankind. They, by identification with the processes of continuous creation, are themselves fashioners of other complete men. Some talk, others are silent, some walk it seems restlessly, others sit

and teach. To understand them you must bring into action
an intelligence which is an intuitive one ...

What, then, *is* the 'completeness' that the Sufi refers to, and in
what way are we incomplete? Only the Sufi adept himself is in
a position to fully understand these questions. Nevertheless, it
is possible to say something on the subject.

Sufis say that we are 'asleep' in some way. In fact their word
for man is 'the sleeper'. Our present consciousness is but a dim
shadow of the full consciousness possible to us if we awaken.
'For now we see through a glass, darkly; but then face to face;' as
Paul, or rather William Tyndale, the poet translator of our Bible,
puts it. And as Jesus himself, among his many references to 'sleep'
both in his parables and elsewhere, says: 'Awake, thou that sleepest,
and arise from the dead, and Christ shall give thee light.'

According to the Sufis, man has dormant perceptions of
which he is not aware, hidden faculties waiting to be developed. The light of his possible higher consciousness lies hidden under his 'bushel'[2]—as the Nazarene master expressed it.
In his relative unconsciousness lies his incompleteness. To be
complete means to be conscious, completely conscious. It also
means to be re-attached inwardly to the Source of Being and
of Wisdom, God, from whom we have been separated. We can
then become true participants in the Universe, the real and
spiritual Universe—to which we ultimately belong.

'Sufism', says the great Sufi teacher Rumi, 'is the effort of
man to re-unite with the understanding from which he has
been cut off.'

The following quotation from the statement by the master
Ustad Hilmi, entitled *The Sufi Quest*, is valuable both as a description of the Sufi Way and with regard to the role of teachers in this
field such as Jesus, Moses, and others less publicly known:

Man, we say we know, originates from far away; so far,
indeed, that in speaking of his origin, such phrases as

'beyond the stars' are frequently employed. Man is estranged from his origins. Some of his feelings (but not all of them) are slight indicators of this.

Man has the opportunity of returning to his origin. He has forgotten this. He is, in fact, 'asleep' to the reality.

Sufism is designed as the means to help awaken man to the realisation, not just the opinion, of the above statements. Those who waken are able to return, to start 'the journey', while also living this present life in all its fullness. Traditions about monasticism and isolation are reflections of short-term processes of training or development, monstrously misunderstood and grotesquely elaborated to provide refuges for those who want to stay asleep ... Since Sufism depends upon effectiveness, not belief, Sufis are not concerned with inculcating and maintaining belief.

If man finds himself again, he will be able to increase his existence infinitely. If he does not, he may dwindle to vanishing point.

People have been sent, from time to time, to try to serve man and save him from the 'blindness' and 'sleep' (which today would be better described as 'amnesia') which is always described in our technical literature as a local disease. These people are always in touch with the Origin, and they bring the 'medicine' which is half the cure. The other half, as in orthodox terrestrial medicine, is the activity of that which is acted upon, to attain its own regeneration with the minimum of aid .... They have been of all raccs, and they have belonged to all faiths.

Numerous residual systems for human progress continue to float around in the world, but virtually all are devoid of value in this inner aspect, though they may not be without historical interest .... They can most charitably be described as vehicles abandoned by their builders and now occupied by half-comprehending amateurs who seek only a relief from thought about their predicament.

This symbolic illustration, Plate One of the anonymous 17th century alchemical text, the *Mutus Liber*, speaks for itself. Ascending and descending angels, representing spiritually advanced beings, are attempting to awaken the sleeping man to his potential consciousness. The reference is to Jacob's Ladder, connecting Earth to Heaven.

Genesis 28.12

Recognising a 'True Master' is possible only when the postulant, man or woman, is what we call 'sincere'. This technical term refers to his condition, not his opinions.

Sufism has two main technical objectives: (1) to show the man himself as he really is; and (2) to help him develop his real, inner self, his permanent part.

Though man 'originates from far away, is asleep and may return after he has attained the means' he can do so only if he works from a sound environmental base in the world in which we find him: our slogan is 'Be in the World, but not of the World'.

Though Hilmi says: 'They have been of all races, and they have belonged to all faiths', it is also true that many teachers of this kind have not been associated with any religion at all. This is because the essence of this activity is spiritual rather than religious, concerned with experience rather than belief. For while belief binds, experience liberates. It is relevant that the word 'religion' is derived from the Latin *religere*—to bind. Sufism therefore is not a religion. Development—the development of human understanding—is very different to indoctrination, religious or otherwise.

Thus even those Sufis who have been associated with, or have founded what are termed 'religions', have understood and employed their concepts in a special way. While conscious of the ethical interpretation of some of their teachings, valid as far as it goes, they are primarily concerned with the communication of inner dimensions of meaning. So they create schools for the transmission of the inner or esoteric element of their teaching for those with the necessary desire and receptivity for such education. 'He that has ears to hear—let him hear,' as Jesus repeatedly puts it.

There is every indication to suggest that Jesus of Nazareth was the founder of just such a school, of Master and disciples. He was a teacher with his students—*discipulus* means pupil or student, not 'follower', which is the abject and passive notion resulting from the orthodox Christian image of Jesus as some kind of god to be worshipped. No, Jesus did not encourage personality-worship any more than any Sufi teacher has ever done. Thus, when someone addresses him as 'Good Master' he abruptly replies: 'Why callest thou me good? There is none good but God.'[3] He was involved in education, not adulation. And like all Sufi teachers he was aware that the latter interfered with the former. 'Look not at my face, but take what is in my hand.' says Rumi. According to the Sufis, awe prevents communication.

'The Sufis affirm that the organism known generally as Sufism has been the one stream of direct, evolutionary experience which has been the determining factor in all the great schools of mysticism.' Says the contemporary Sufi, Idries Shah, in his study of the manifestations and meaning of this activity, *The Sufis*. While the eleventh-century teacher Hujwiri, in his classic text *Revelation of the Veiled* maintains: 'Sufism has no history, as other things have a history. It can be said to have existed always.'

There is no contradiction between the two statements. The earlier master is simply stressing the extra-temporal nature of the source of Sufi activity. Its origin and essence are timeless. It emerges from eternity, from time to time—into time. 'My kingdom is not of this world,' said Jesus, expressing the same truth.

Thus all true inner schools are projected by, and linked to, the same extra-dimensional source. 'Our objective is to achieve, by the understanding of the Origin, the Knowledge which comes through experience', states Hamadani, another eleventh-century Sufi.

Nevertheless, due to inadequate information on, and superficial study of, the matter, a widespread notion still persists that Sufism is 'Islamic mysticism'. This assumption has understandably arisen from the fact that for centuries there has been a clear and continuing Sufi presence within several Islamic countries, and a number of their great masters have lived and operated in the Middle East. But, as has been said, the Sufi Teaching transcends all religions, and is not culture-bound. It addresses the spiritual element in all mankind.

Thus, when Rumi died (in 1273) his funeral was attended by a very variegated collection of people—of all faiths, or none. A Christian priest present was asked why he wept so bitterly at the death of a Moslem teacher. He replied: 'We esteem him as the Moses, the David, the Jesus of the age. We are all his followers and disciples.' This remark, observes Shah, 'shows the Sufi idea of recurrence of teaching and of the transmission of spiritual activity'. The disciple who made it was clearly aware of all the men he had mentioned as different exponents of the same ongoing Tradition. And aware, too, that though the teaching was recurrent, it is to the present expression of it that one has to relate.

Rumi himself has this to say on the subject:

> I am no Christian, no Jew, no Magian, no Musulman
> Not of the East, not of the West.
> Not of the land, not of the sea
> My place placeless, my trace traceless.[4]

He was indicating that transcendent level of being which his Christian disciple had grasped in his own way. This was the level where all masters are 'one'—a level which Jesus shared with Rumi, and through which he could thus contact 'Jesus'.

In his great work *Wisdom of Illumination* the twelfth-century Sufi master Suhrawardi specifically states that 'the Sufi philosophy is identical with the inner teachings of all the ancients— the Egyptians, the Persians, the Greeks, and is the knowledge of Light and the deepest truth, through which man can attain to a state about which he cannot normally even dream.'

The following century, Roger Bacon, who was signifi- canly both Franciscan and Sufi, makes a similar statement in his

Philosophia Occulta, where he claims that this knowledge was known to Noah and Abraham, to the Chaldean and Egyptian masters, to Zoroaster and Hermes, certain Greek sages including Pythagoras, Anaxagoras and Socrates, and to the Sufis.

Roger Bacon, while nominally a Christian as a member of the Franciscan Order, is reputed to have lectured at Oxford, in Arab dress, on the Sufi philosophy.

How was this possible? The answer is that this Order was not all it appeared to be, despite its acceptance by the Church. It is more than probable that in its conception and during its early history it was a disguised Sufi organisation.

There is much evidence for this, collected and presented by Shah in his chapter on Francis of Assisi in *The Sufis.* Suffice it to say here that before founding his Order in about 1223 Francis made two journeys, one to the East and one to Morocco, both inexplicable to his biographers. Shah believes that he, as a troubadour, was engaged in establishing contact with the source of the inspiration of his troubadour poetry. That this was Sufic is fairly certain, as the considerable research into the subject by Ernest Scott in his *People of the Secret* indicates.

As for the Sufi influence upon the nature of his Order as a whole, Shah observes:

> The atmosphere and setting of the Franciscan Order is closer to a dervish organisation than anything else. Apart from the tales about St. Francis which are held in common with Sufi teachers, all kinds of points coincide. The special methodology of what Francis calls 'holy prayer' indicates an affinity with the dervish 'remembering', quite apart from the whirling (*sic*). The dress of the Order, with its hooded cloak and wide sleeves, is that of the dervishes of Morocco and Spain.

A point of peculiar interest that must be mentioned is that Najmuddin Kubra, who founded the Sufi order called the

Greater Brethren, contemporary with St. Francis, was known to have had an uncanny influence over animals. Pictures always show him surrounded by birds of all kinds. We all know that Francis himself was famous for his ability to communicate with animals, and it is recorded that he delivered sermons to an audience of birds. It is also significant that the early Franciscans called themselves the 'Lesser Brethren'. A connection with the Kubravi order is difficult to avoid.

Here we have a highly intelligent and cultured Western man, Francis of Assisi, who, although reared in the religious context of Catholic Christendom, recognises that it is a spiritually derelict relic of a once living teaching, that of Jesus, whose source he identifies as the Sufi tradition. In connection with this source he thereupon sets about a limited rescue and revival operation, taking the form of the Franciscan Order.

Esoteric Christianity, therefore, which Jesus taught, was but one manifestation, one projection, one facet, of Sufism, the essence of esotericism.

He and his disciples did not of course call the teaching 'Christianity'—a term which first appeared many years later—but referred to it as 'the way'[5] in accordance with Sufi and mystical practice, to express simultaneously the concept of a journey to be travelled or path to be followed, and a method by which something is to be done.

It was not until A.D. 45, when Paul and Barnabas were on a mission to Antioch, that the term 'Christian' was first coined—and by the people of that city. As we read in Acts 11.26: 'And the disciples were called Christians first in Antioch.'

The inhabitants of that city can hardly be regarded as having been experts in the important matter of nomenclature! But whether Paul and Barnabas liked it or not the name stuck.

It is unlikely that the term was ever accepted by the inner group of disciples, under James' leadership, at Jerusalem. This was the centre. Here were the authentic representatives, the true continuers of the teaching. Compared to them, the original twelve, Paul was a newcomer at the periphery, and not a disciple in the real sense, which is why they were always reluctant to recognise him as such.

With regard to the term 'Christianity' it is nowhere to be found in New Testament literature. The first record of its use is by Ignatius, Bishop of Antioch, in his letter to the Magnesians in A.D. 107. It tends to imply a completed and static body of doctrine, while the concept 'way' expresses a dynamic current of activity *in a certain direction.*

Which is why the original school of Jesus used this term to describe the special developmental education they were engaged upon—in common with general Sufi practice. It was a way within the Way, the great Sufi Way, the Ancient Path to Wisdom. For wisdom can only be an organic aspect of inner growth. Otherwise it cannot be 'contained'—as Jesus explains (John 16.12): 'I have yet many things to say unto you but ye cannot contain them now.' A new 'receiving organ' has to be developed. Which is why 'No man putteth new wine into old bottles.' (Mark 2.22).

Our mystical poet William Blake knew exactly what Jesus meant. Under one of his paintings appear the lines:

> The Sun's Light when he unfolds it
> Depends on the organ that beholds it.

He was talking about that necessary correlation between knowledge and being, well understood by the ancients but lost sight of by our modern culture and so-called philosophy—that knowledge depends on being. 'To be and to know are one and the same', said Parmenides (about 510 BC), while Plato is expressing the same truth in his parable of 'The Cave'. In it prisoners are chained so as to face the back wall of a cave with their backs to the entrance and the Sun beyond. Behind them is a fire, and between it and them pass men carrying various objects, whose shadows are cast upon the wall before them. It is a life-sentence, so all they ever see are the reflections of things. However, occasionally one of the prisoners manages to break his bonds, turn and face the light. He then sees things as they really are.

What this says about the human condition we must all decide for ourselves.

In Plato's own interpretation of it he comments: 'The instrument of knowledge has to be turned around to the things of being, till the soul is able, by degrees, to support the light of true being, and can look at the brightest.'

'Unless ye turn, ye cannot enter the Kingdom,' says Jesus. Returning to Blake:

> If the doors of perception were cleansed
> Everything would appear to man as it is, infinite
> For man has closed himself up,
> Till he sees all things
> Through the narrow chink of his cavern.

He is obviously talking about the same cave as Plato. Elsewhere Blake says: 'As a man is, so he sees,' which makes it clear that he is as aware as the Greek philosophers that knowledge depends upon being—that they are organically interrelated.

As, for example, an ant cannot see beyond an ant's level of being, that is, further than the limits of intelligence inherent in the level of its being; and a cat similarly cannot transcend the potentiality of its own particular being, so likewise a human being cannot perceive beyond the capacity of perception that corresponds with the level of being he or she has reached. We are talking then of something that could be described as a gradient of 'being-knowledge'.

This concept is central to Sufism, and also to the teaching of Gurdjieff, who appears to have had considerable contact with the Sufis. He said: 'Within the limits of a given level of being the quality of knowledge cannot be changed.' Note the accent on quality rather than quantity—something that modern man has not yet grasped. In other words the quality of being governs the quality of knowledge.

I'd like to quote Gurdjieff again on this subject, bearing in mind that he embraced a wider spectrum of life than the one recognised by the current paradigm. He is talking about 'people':

> 'Being' for them means simply 'existence'. They do not understand that being or existence may be of very different levels or categories. Take for instance the being of a mineral and of a plant. It is a different being. The being of a plant and of an animal is again a different being. The being of an animal and of a man is a different being. But the being of two people can differ from one another more than the being of a mineral and of an animal. This is exactly what people do not understand. And they do not understand that knowledge depends on being. Not only do they not understand this latter—but they definitely do not wish to understand it.

However, if Gurdjieff is wrong and some of us do want to understand it, and are open to the possibility of varying levels of being within humanity, then we can begin to recognise such statements as 'I have yet many things to say unto you, but ye cannot contain them now' and 'No man putteth new wine into old bottles' as the technical language of a practising teacher of the knowledge that only comes with the increase of one's very being.

Notes

1. The actual term used by the Sufis, *Insan-i-Kamil*, is more accurately rendered as 'the completed man'.
2. 'A drum is not beaten under a coverlet' (Sufi saying).
3. Mark 10. 18.
4. From his *Divan-i-Shams-i-Tabriz*.
5. See Matthew 22.16, or Acts 9.2.

CHAPTER TWO

The kingdom of heaven

It is clear from the Gospels that the whole aim and object of Jesus' teaching was to enter 'the kingdom of heaven'. This was the term he used for that higher state of being and consciousness, that 'life more abundant', for which we have the potential, and which is the possession of the completed human being. But as we are now, we are incomplete, hence our deep unease and sense of unfulfilment. This will continue until we do what we were ultimately created for—enter the kingdom.

Though this is our birthright it is not an automatic inheritance, not a 'natural' endowment. It has to be striven for,[1] under guidance. Such guidance comes from a teacher, like Jesus, who directs the effort of the student, making it, as the Sufis say, 'right effort'. Such help is both subtle and sophisticated. And obviously indispensable. It is not enough to want to 'overcome the world' which Jesus says we must do to enter 'the kingdom'. We must also know *how* to overcome the world, and recognise it when we see it. This requires education. For 'the world' is the technical term used by the Sufis for 'everything that weighs down the soul'. Needless to say, there are quite a number of things that weigh down the soul—and some are not as obvious as others. A sense of discernment in this respect must be developed.

> And when he was demanded of the Pharisees, when the kingdom of God should come, he answered them and said, The kingdom of God cometh not with observation:
>
> Neither shall they say, Lo, here! or There! for lo, the kingdom of God is within you.

Here the inner nature of 'the kingdom' is made dramatically clear—in contrast to the uselessness of looking outwardly or externally for it, which is meant by 'observation'[2] Another statement by Jesus on this subject is one of the very interesting 'Oxyrhynchus' Sayings on papyrus discovered in Egypt in 1897, on the site of the ancient city of Oxyrhynchus.

> Who then are they that draw us, and when shall come the kingdom that is in heaven?
>
> The fowls of the air and of the beasts whatever is beneath the earth or upon the earth, and the fishes of the sea, these they are that draw you.
>
> And the Kingdom of heaven is within you and whosoever knoweth himself shall find it. And having found it, ye shall know yourselves that ye are the sons and heirs of the Father, the Almighty, and shall know yourselves that ye are in God and God in you. And ye are the City of God

This saying is one of many that, for one reason or another, have been excluded from the four gospels we are familiar with. The reason may have been that such material was incomprehensible to, or otherwise inconsistent with, the perception of Christianity held by their writers. This is of obvious significance for our understanding of the Master's teaching.

We learn from it that a prerequisite for entry into the Kingdom is a certain kind of self-knowledge—'knowing yourself'. And also that he or she who attains this state of self-knowing becomes a 'son' or 'daughter' of God. Which of course throws much light on the meaning of 'son of God' as applied to Jesus himself.

Here too Jesus places himself firmly and clearly in the direct line of ancient wisdom teaching that has graced the great cultures of both East and West for thousands of years. This is the teaching that left its imprint in the inscription 'Know Thyself' above the entrance to the Delphic Oracle, that ever-living Way whose perennial exponents are the Sufis.

We will now look at the version of this parable which appears at the beginning of the *Gospel of Thomas*, discovered with forty-nine other early works, in the sands of Upper Egypt near Nag Hammadi in 1945. This remarkable document contains one hundred and fourteen sayings and parables of Jesus, many of which have never been seen before. Jesus said

> If those who lead you say to you:
> 'See, the Kingdom is in the sky,'
> then the birds will reach it before you.
> If they say to you: 'It is in the sea,'
> then the fish will precede you.
> But the Kingdom is within you and it is
> without you.
> If you know yourselves,
> then you will be known,
> you will know that you are the sons and daughters
> of the Living Father.
> But if you do not know yourselves
> then you are in poverty—
> and you are poverty.'

This beautiful and powerful parable consummately communicates the inwardness of the Kingdom and the importance of correct orientation towards it. The way lies within.

It is significant, too, that the Aramaic word translated as 'kingdom'—*markuth*—and the Greek word *basileia* both have the sense of 'realm' or 'sphere of influence', rather than 'place'. The Kingdom of God is thus the inner realm of the Universe reached by God's Radiance, the plane of His Power. This is expressed in the earlier Oxyrhynchus version by the words:

> And ye shall know yourselves that ye are in God and God in you. And ye are the City of God.

It is impossible not to be reminded of the wonderful verses of Francis Thompson:

> Does the fish soar to find the ocean
> The eagle plunge to find the air—
> That we ask of the stars in motion
> If they have rumour of thee there?

> Not where the wheeling systems darken,
> And our benumbed conceiving soars!—
> The drift of pinions, would we hearken,
> Beats at our own clay-shuttered doors.

> The angels keep their ancient places—
> Turn but a stone and start a wing!
> 'Tis ye, 'tis your estranged faces,
> That miss the many-splendoured thing.

The kingdom as mystery

Jesus describes the Kingdom of Heaven as a 'mystery' or 'mysteries'. At Mark 4.11 he tells his disciples:

> Unto you it is given to know the mysteries of the kingdom of heaven: but unto them that are outside all these things are done in parables ...[3]

26

Three Worlds, by M. C. Escher
The fish symbolises another consciousness lying below
the surface of the ordinary consciousness. Interestingly,
the Fish was the secret symbol of early Christians.

According to the Sufis a 'mystery' is the special esoteric technical term to denote 'a change of perception and understanding', or stage in the development of being and consciousness reached by the follower of the spiritual path.

It is clear that Jesus was using the word in this sense, a sense shared by the Mystery Schools whose traditional language he was speaking. A *mystes* for them was someone who had been initiated into the mysteries. The common aim they shared with the school of Jesus was that transformation of being which they variously termed 'rebirth' or 'resurrection'. It is not surprising to learn that the contemporary Mystery Schools regarded 'the Christian Mysteries'as of their kind.

In *The Books of the Saviour*, the extracanonical text discovered by Askew in Egypt in 1785, we find the following statement by Jesus:

> For this cause therefore have I brought keys of the mysteries of the kingdom of heaven: otherwise no flesh in the world will be saved. For without mysteries no-one will enter into the Light Kingdom, whether he be righteous or doer of wrong.

He here makes unequivocally clear that entry into the kingdom depends on mystical rather than moral quality. Knowledge of the mysteries is essential.

This is not to lessen the importance of morality. It is simply that it is not enough. And ultimately a real understanding of ethics can only come from an evolution of consciousness. Only thus can a true knowledge of right and wrong be obtained. Only thus can one see what one is really doing. The development of consciousness is also the development of conscience. They are one.

It is as well at this stage to clarify the meaning of 'esoteric' in view of common misunderstandings surrounding the term. It is derived from the Greek *esoteros* which means 'inner'. By this is meant that which pertains to, or is perceivable by, the inner perceptions. If it is therefore hidden, it is not so deliberately, but by virtue of its very nature. Being inner it is accessible only to the inner faculties, and thus hidden to, or out of sight of, the 'outer' or exoteric faculties. If it is 'secret', it is intrinsically secret. As the Sufis say: 'The secret protects itself.'

It is all a matter of perception. Which is why Jesus constantly says: 'He that hath ears to hear, let him hear.'[4]

Notes

1. 'To him that *overcometh*, God shall give to eat of the Tree of Life'. (Revelations 2.7).
2. The Greek word thus translated is *paratereseos*—literally 'looking *outside*'.
3. 'We remember our Lord and Teacher, how he charged us, saying: "Ye shall keep my mysteries for me and the sons of my house." '—a saying of Jesus recorded by Clement of Alexandria in his *Stomateis*.
4. 'It is with the heart that one hears.'—*Brihadaranyaka Upanishad* 1, 5, 3.

CHAPTER THREE

The initiatory way

The practice or process known as 'initiation' is of common, central significance to all mystical schools and nothing is more surrounded by mystery, secrecy and misunderstanding. As we have already discussed initiation implies an inner human change that is 'secret' or esoteric by virtue of its very nature. The 'secret' of transformation cannot be told. It can only be experienced.

There is no such thing as instantaneous initiation. It is always and only the result of long work on oneself, together with special help—the help of the 'initiator'. This, as has already been said, is the superior being or teacher responsible, who not only guides the student or seeker in all manner of ways, empowering him or her to follow the path by virtue of a special power he possesses, but also actually elevates the seeker's very being and consciousness by some kind of direct spiritual transmission. The Sufis refer to this power as *Baraka*.

The three stages of initiation

From ancient times esoteric schools have identified three stages or 'degrees' of initiation. This is certainly so of Jesus, and the Sufis generally—as we shall see.

At Eleusis the first stage was called *katharsis*, which means 'purification'; the second *telete*, meaning 'initiation'; and the last was *epopteia*, or 'vision'. They were thus a sequence of ascending levels of development.

It is significant that Clement of Alexandria, the teacher of a school of esoteric Christianity in that city towards the end of the second century, used exactly these terms—*katharsis, telete* and *epopteia*—to describe the progression of states possible to a student of the way. Thus, he said, would 'the mysteries' be experienced, leading ultimately to 'Gnosis'. Clement claimed, like the Gnostics, to be in contact with the inner tradition of Jesus' teaching—of which the Church outside was ignorant.[1]

The terms Jesus actually used to refer to the three successive initiations or 'baptisms' were Water, Air, and Fire. This was also the symbology of the later alchemists of the Middle Ages, as it was of the ancient Greek sages Thales, Anaximander, and Anaximenes—whose profound and sophisticated thought, like that of the alchemists, has been so misunderstood by modern one-dimensional literalist interpreters.

Jesus' leading statement on the subject is at John 3.5: 'Except a man be born of water, and of the spirit, he cannot enter the Kingdom of God.' Now place alongside this John the Baptist's previous announcement: 'I indeed baptise you with water; but he that cometh after me shall baptise you with spirit, and with fire'. Bearing in mind that the Greek word *pneuma* here translated as 'spirit' also has the meaning 'air', we can see clearly that both teachers are using the same symbolic language of 'The Four Elements': Earth, Water, Air and Fire. The Kingdom of God referred to by Jesus is thus equivalent to the final element, or state, of Fire. This is borne out by other remarks by Jesus about 'fire', but is nowhere more clearly highlighted than in this saying attributed to him by

Origen and other early witnesses—but not recorded in the familiar Gospels:

> He that is near to me is near the fire. He that is far from me
> is far from the Kingdom.

The baptism of 'fire'[2] is therefore that high state of being which connects man with the Divine, which enables him to enter the Kingdom of Consciousness, and makes him a 'citizen of Heaven'. Transformed into his true self he can play a true and deep role in the unfolding Universe—as a colleague of his Creator. Therein lies his destiny.

Sufic use of the 'Four Elements' symbology

The Sufis employ this symbology to express the ascending sequences of stages in the development of consciousness possible to man, and enable us to understand more clearly what Jesus and his pupils were doing. I quote from two texts, one *The Meaning of the Path* by Qalimi, the other *A Coptic Conception of Initiation and Illumination* by the Christian Sufi, Maryam H. Ghali, bringing them into parallel:

> *Ghali*: The way of initiation is a term used to describe the method by which one can attain, under certain circumstances, to a real consciousness of truth. The Way must begin with an individual who has travelled the Way. He is the guide or shepherd whose task it is to conduct others to the end of the road.

> *Qalimi*: The Way of Initiation, in which an individual can reach, if his desire is pure, the status possible to him, has been called the Idkhal, the Causing to Enter (on the Way). The Way has three parts. It must begin with an individual who has already travelled the Way. This individual must come into contact with those who are at the lowest

stage, in order to conduct them higher. The lowest stage is called Earth. The other stages, successively, are known as Water, Air and Fire.

We then get extremely helpful information by both authorities on what happens at the stage of 'water':

> *Ghali*: The stage of water, as distinct from earth, marks a very significant period in the development of consciousness: ... water (the subtler and purer part of the human being) can be mixed with water (the subtler and purer element of a higher consciousness). This means that 'water', the purer part of the person concerned, can be brought into a true mixture or relationship with the higher 'substances' of the spiritual world. The baptist is the person charged with this task, and capable of it, the task to help raise higher the consciousness so that it may be able to amalgamate with the consciousness of divine truth at its lowest level.
>
> The baptism of water, therefore, which was as far as John the Baptist, according to his own words, was authorised to confer, was the preparatory stage of giving the individual the potentiality for a further development.

> *Qalimi*: The stage of 'Water', also symbolising 'purification' in some traditions, takes place when the Teacher is in a position to amalgamate[3] the watery (that is the mobile and purified) element in the postulant with 'water' in another sense. This latter 'water' is a finer substance of a spiritual kind, partaking of the nature of an energy. When this is possible, a certain kind of 'mobility' can take place.

Maryam Ghali then tells us something of 'the baptism of Air' in Christianity, having explained that: 'In the Semitic languages, originally used by the Old and New Testament figures, the term for spirit is the same as the word for Air, (Ruah).' This means, she says, that a person 'has reached a second stage of inner understanding of the divine, characterised by the stage of the spirit.' Such is 'the higher, mystical 'baptism of Air'.

She refers us to John the Baptist's statement at Matthew 3.11: 'I indeed baptise you with water; But he that cometh after me shall baptise you with spirit, and with fire.'

Qalimi informs: '"Water" cannot truly purify without the deliberate effort of the person to be cleansed. As the degrees proceed, the effort becomes greater. Although the effort may appear continuous or otherwise, the true harmonisation which is taking place at each stage requires the correct attunement of all the members of a group (taifa, halqa) involved.'

He continues: 'The stage of "Air" is reached after completing the "Water" "daraja" (grade). In this, the consciousness of the individual (or the group, if there is one) rises to a perception of true Reality higher than is possible at the "Water" stage.'

Qalimi also gives us significant information about the nature and purpose of a Sufi group. 'Sufis select disciples in such a manner as to enable one to affect the other and make the process more effective. Hence study groups when indicated. The Sufic "current" can also be conveyed between members of a group who do not formally meet.'

After a further development beyond the stage of 'Air' it is possible, says Qalimi, with the help of a Teacher, to reach the final level of 'Fire'. 'This, highest, consciousness—gnosis—is represented in ordinary words as contact with the Divine. This is the stage also referred to as the 'Death before death'. Jesus refers to this when he says:

> Except a corn of wheat fall into the ground and die, it abideth alone; but if it die, it bringeth forth much fruit. (John 12.24)

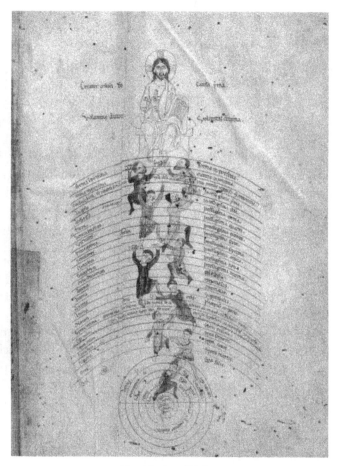

The Chain of Being

This diagram, illustrates the concept of a continuum or chain of being
from man to God, now lost to Christianity but once understood as
essential to the whole operation of spiritual develpment. It makes clear
the different levels of being possible to humanity, and the necessity
of help for each level above it. Note that each of these human figures
stretches out his hand to the one above him. The ilustration is from a
twelfth-century manuscript in the Bibliothèque Nationale, Paris.

Maryam Ghali says of this highest state of refinement: 'the term being used for what has formerly been called the "baptism of fire" is also the term "The Kingdom of God" '. She further says of this Kingdom that it is 'within man: his innermost consciousness; the link with the divine.'

The co-incidence at all points between the statements of the Sufi, Qalimi, and the Christian Sufi, Maryam Ghali, makes it clear that we are dealing with the same Tradition.

A final observation: When quoting the verse 'Except a man be born of water, and the spirit, he cannot enter the kingdom of God' (John 3.5), Ghali comments that 'baptisms are also known and spoken of currently, as in all initiatory or esoteric systems, as 'rebirths'. This was indeed so of the Mystery Schools, where the initiated seeker was described as *renatus*—reborn into a higher kind of life and consciousness. Thus in the text entitled *The Liturgy of Mithra* from the Mithraic Mysteries we read:

> Today I have been born again by Thee, out of all the myriads,
> For the life-giving rebirth.

Qalimi might not directly speak of 'rebirth', but implies it in 'the death before death'. What is certain is that Sufis maintain that 'the self' in its development has to pass through a number of processes termed 'death and rebirth'.

Throughout the description of this ascending spiritual sequence we are made aware of the need for the initiator, the human helper who has been that way already. He or she is that most especial communicator. Though he can only help those who help themselves. We will conclude with a statement from Ghali:

> The Sufis, who are often called esoteric Christians, partly because they revere Jesus as a master of the Way, continue

to practise the three degrees of communication of consciousness. They do this by a variety of methods, all designed to communicate to the individual and the group the illumination of truth at a level corresponding to the stage which that individual and group have reached.

An interesting document, believed to be a fragment of a letter by Clement of Alexandria, was discovered in 1973. It indicates the existence of an expanded version of Mark's Gospel, written by the disciple himself for the use of special pupils of the esoteric school of Alexandria, who were following the initiatory teaching:

> Mark, then, during Peter's stay in Rome, he wrote (an account of) the Lord's doings, not however declaring all (of them), nor yet hinting at the secret (ones), but selecting those he thought most useful for increasing the faith of those being instructed. But when Peter died as a martyr, Mark came over to Alexandria, bringing both his own notes and those of Peter, from which he transferred to his former book the things suitable to whatever makes for progress toward knowledge (gnosis). Thus he composed a more spiritual Gospel for the use of those who were being perfected. Nevertheless he did not divulge the things not to be uttered, nor did he write down the hierophantic teaching of the Lord, but to the stories already written he added others and, moreover, brought in certain ways of which he knew the interpretation would, as a mystagogue, lead his hearers into the innermost sanctuary of that truth hidden by seven veils. Thus, in sum, he prearranged matters, neither grudgingly nor incautiously, in my opinion, and dying, he left his composition to the church in Alexandria, where it even yet is most carefully guarded, being read only to those who are being initiated into the great mysteries.[4]

Such documents as the one referred to here not only yield levels of meaning according to the levels of the recipients, but also conduct *to* such levels.

Notes

1. What appears to be an authentic fragment of a letter by Clement has recently been discovered (by Morton Smith) and is quoted at the end of the chapter.

2. 'Amen. I say unto you I have brought down water and fire from the Treasure of Light'—saying of Jesus in the Gnostic text *The Book of the Saviour*.

   'If the mortal draws near the fire he shall have Light from God.' (*The Chaldean Oracles*). Significantly, the ancient Greek philosopher Heraclitus (501 BC) seems to have held the same concept: 'All comes from and returns to Fire.' (*The Cosmic Fragments*).

   Thus the declaration at Luke XII.49: 'I am come to send fire on the earth; and what will I if it be already kindled? But I have a baptism to be baptised with; and how am I straitened till it be accomplished?' is clearly of alchemical intent.

3. 'There is a mingling that leadeth unto death, and a mingling that leadeth unto life'—*Book of the Saviour* (Gnostic Text).

4. Morton Smith, *Clement of Alexandria and a Secret Gospel of Mark*, Harper & Row 1973, page 17.

CHAPTER FOUR

Gnosis

'Gnosis' is the ancient Greek word for 'knowledge', but the esoteric and spiritual meaning is not what is ordinarily meant by knowledge but something deeper than that, a perception of the whole nature of the Universe, inner and outer, and how one integrates with it and its evolution.

This relationship, this *engagement* with the Universe seen and unseen is what the ancient schools calling themselves 'The Gnostics' must have meant by the term 'Gnosis' which was their aim to attain. It was transcendental knowledge, only to be acquired by special education and effort.

The normal condition of man, according to the Gnostics is one of 'agnoia' or ignorant sleep, a state into which he has fallen, unconscious of his origin, identity and destiny. He has become hypnotised by the world, which he takes to be the only world, and suffers from a kind of amnesia. He has to awake and return to himself, his true self, and re-unite with the Universe and its Creator. Appropriately the Gnostics called this state 'The Reunion'.

While the great Sufi teacher Rumi describes Sufism as 'the effort of man to reunite with the understanding from which he has been cut off'. The Gnostic teacher Valentinus quotes Jesus as saying: 'Seek and ye shall receive a return.' He goes on to explain that 'return' as a 'return to consciousness', and adds that 'in the reunion each one shall receive himself'.

In this context one cannot but be reminded of Jesus' story of a certain prodigal who 'having journeyed into a far country, and there wasted his substance' finally 'came to himself' and returned to his father (Luke 15). Tyndale's original translation is: 'Then he remembered hymsilfe'. Which will be of interest to students of Gurdjieff.

Perhaps the most explicit reference by Jesus to knowledge is this saying which for one reason or another does not appear in the Bible:

> Verily I say unto you, he who has not been born twice will not see the kingdom of the heavens and the earth. The first birth is the birth of nature, and the second birth is the birth of the spirit in the heaven of knowledge.

The knowledge Jesus is referring to must be gnosis.

In fact the word 'gnosis' occurs in the original Greek New Testament no less than 19 times. Yet Christianity as it is generally understood—or misunderstood—has settled for belief rather than knowledge. In fact it doesn't believe *in* knowledge. Of a higher, transcendental order, that is. There can be no such thing as gnosis.

It was not always like this. Listen to Paul in his First Letter to the Corinthians:

> This is wisdom we preach among the perfect, yet not the wisdom of this age nor of the leaders of this age, which will become nothing. We preach the wisdom of God, mysterious and hidden, which was foreordained by God before all ages for our glory, a wisdom which none of the leaders of our age have ever known.

And again, in his Letter to the Ephesians:

> That ye being rooted and grounded may be able to com-
> prehend with all saints what is the breadth and length,
> and depth and height.

Here Paul is clearly indicating that he is aware of the possibility for man of another, higher mode of consciousness in
which he can perceive and participate in other dimensions of
the Universe. He is of course talking about gnosis.

In his earlier statement he speaks of 'the wisdom of God,
mysterious and hidden, which was foreordained by God
before all ages for our glory ...' This concurs with the insight of
the Gnostic teacher Valentinus who says in *The Gospel of Truth*
(circa 170 AD):

> The Father, who withholds within Himself their complete-
> ness, Gives it to them as a return to Himself, and a Gnosis.

Both Paul and Valentinus, the latter claiming access to an inner
Christian tradition, see human growth in terms of the claiming
of an inheritance, the receiving of a 'withheld' birthright.

But this birthright has to be worked for, deserved. As the
Sufi master Haraadani explains:

> Our objective is to achieve, by the understanding of
> the Origin, the Knowledge which comes through expe-
> rience. This is done, as with a journey, only with those
> who already know the Way. The justice of this state is
> the greatest justice of all: because while this knowledge
> cannot be withheld from him who deserves it, it cannot
> be given to him who does not deserve it. It is the only
> substance with a discriminating faculty of its own, inher-
> ent justice.

There is, it appears, a track through the Universe that awaits each one of us. And help available to follow it. 'Seek and you shall be found,' say the Sufis. 'Knock and it shall be opened unto you,' says Jesus.

Now what can we say about the nature of the intelligence called gnosis? By all accounts it is intuitive. But it is a highly and deeply developed intuition. Of a different order of magnitude. Like a fire to a flame. The Sufis call it 'Direct Perception'. It connects one's consciousness with a Cosmic Plan. It engages one with the Pattern.

That Pattern is always moving, so the comprehension that relates to it must be moving too. Thus gnosis is better described as *knowing*, a constantly shifting knowing, rather than knowledge, which tends to imply something static. Though undoubtedly there do exist eternal truths. So gnosis is best thought of as having both static and dynamic elements. One could perhaps think in terms of an 'organ' of gnosis deep within us, waiting to be developed, called by both Jesus and the Sufis 'the heart', which is a *touchstone* to what is Right in every sense of the word, ethical, spiritual and evolutionary in a given situation. An inner compass oriented to the Cosmic context. An immediate perception of the *essence* of a situation—how to be and what to do in it to serve the Universe, mankind, and oneself.

CHAPTER FIVE

Son of God

Jesus never used the term 'son of God' to describe himself, though it was occasionally used of him by others. He referred to himself as 'the son of man'. There is little doubt that this concept has an esoteric dimension, but without the help of the master its ultimate meaning cannot be ascertained. It seems fair to assume, however, that one reason why he selected it was to stress his humanity, the common humanity he shared with us all—in addition to the uncommon humanity which could be shared with those willing to work for it. The term appears simultaneously to express 'representative man', and 'man the herald of man to come'.

While the four canonical Gospels contain nothing to help us in understanding 'the son of man', the other Gospels give us revealing indications of its meaning. In the *Gospel of Mary*, discovered in Achmin, Egypt, in 1896, we read:

> Jesus saith:
> Take heed lest anyone lead you astray with the words
> 'Lo here!' or 'Lo there!' for the Son of Man is within you.
> Follow him. Those who seek him will find him.

One is closely reminded of another 'lost' saying of Jesus, recorded and preserved by Al Ghazali: 'Seek ye first yourselves, and all other shall be added unto you.'

Also relevant is this information about the Naassenes, an early Gnostic Christian cult, given by the orthodox churchman Hippolytus in his *Against Heresies* (v.7):

> The Naassenes speak of a nature of man at once hidden and manifesting itself, which they say is within man, and is the kingdom of heaven which is sought after.

Here, taken together with the saying from the *Gospel of Mary*, we have a most significant connection between 'the son of man' and 'the kingdom of heaven'.

> Finally, in the *Gospel of Thomas* (Saying 106):
> Jesus said: 'When you make the two one, you shall become Sons of Man'.

Here the master instructs his disciples (and us) in esoteric psychology, pointing the way to further development. The inner must be joined to the outer, to form the complete man. Essential wholeness is essential. And he says: 'If you bring forth that within yourselves, that which you have will save you' (The 70th saying), referring to the emergence and evolution of the essence. The heart must awake, and arise—the perennial Sufi message.

If we look now at the term 'son of God' as it was used by Jesus and others we will see that it refers to the same state of human being as 'son of man'—but with the accent on the particular relationship to God which this state entails.

From the Sufic point of view it represents a special connection with the Creator, an uplifting and upholding, a return to the Origin—a restoration to one's original being. There, suffused in eternal spiritual power the soul takes up its true level of life. There, identity is not diminished, but increased and intensified by closeness to its Source. Individuality becomes more iridescent, for the nearer we are to God the nearer we are to our selves. Conversely, the nearer we are to our selves, the nearer we are to God.[1] Which is what Jesus meant when he said:

> And the Kingdom of Heaven is within you, and whoso-
> ever knoweth himself shall find it. And having found it,
> ye shall know yourselves that ye are the sons and heirs of
> the Father, the Almighty, and shall know yourselves that
> ye are in God and God in you.

There can be no more unequivocal statement on the nature of a 'son of God'—by one of His sons—than that. He must *know* himself.[2]

In the Sermon on the Mount (Matthew 5.9) Jesus tells us: 'Blessed are the peacemakers, for they shall be called sons of God,' meaning that this state can only be possessed by those who make their own internal peace through self-completion. And at Luke 20.36 he says, referring to this level of humanity: 'Neither can they die any more: for they are equal unto the angels, and are the sons of God being sons of the resurrection.' Resurrection is that inner arising as a result of spiritual work, after a certain kind of 'death', to a higher level or quality of life. It is interesting to notice that the Indian mystic Sarvepalli Radhakrishnan, after studying Christianity, comes to a similar conclusion:

> 'The resurrection is not the rise of the dead from their
> tombs, but the passage from the death of lower self to
> the life of a higher self, from slavery to the world, to the
> liberty of the eternal.'[3]

47

It is clear, too, that Jewish mysticism was familiar with the esoteric implications of the title 'son of God' as this excerpt from one of the *Odes of Solomon*, written anonymously in the century after Jesus, fully indicates:

> 'Although a son of man, I was named Illuminate, the son of God.
>
> For according to the Greatness of the Most High So He made me. He renewed me and He anointed me, And I became one of His neighbours.'[4]

The Gnostic-Sufi Symbol
This symbol indicates the presence of a continuous link between Gnostics who claimed to represent a tradition of esoteric Christian teaching, and a contemporary Sufi school.

In the same century, about 170 AD, the Gnostic teacher Valentinus, claiming access to the inner Christian tradition, expresses the same development as follows:

> The Father, who withholds within Himself their completeness,
> Gives it to them as a return to Himself, and a Gnosis

Here 'gnosis' is spiritual illumination; and human inner growth is seen in terms of the claiming of an inheritance and the receiving of a withheld birthright, that of sonship or daughterhood of God.

Finally, the following statements by John, firstly in his Gospel and then in his Epistle would appear to be another way of saying the same thing. 'But as many as received him, to them gave he power to become sons of God.' (John 1.12)

> Behold what manner of love the Father hath bestowed upon us that we should be called the sons of God.
>
> (First Epistle of John 3.1)

Notes

1. 'To know the Father one must *become* the son.' (Eckhart, the 14th century mystic).
2. It is interesting to study in parallel this saying of Jesus found on the site of Oxyrhynchus, Egypt, in 1897: Jesus saith, '.... If ye shall truly know yourselves, ye are the sons and daughters of the Father Almighty and ye shall know yourselves to be in the City of God, and ye are the City.'

   'Gnosis ... is the mystic knowledge which effects regeneration—rebirth into the full consciousness of one's divine nature and powers as a 'Son of God'.' William Kingsland in *Gnosis or Ancient Wisdom in the Christian Scriptures* (Allen and Unwin, 1937).

49

3. William Kingsland in *Gnosis or Ancient Wisdom in the Christian Scriptures* describes it as 'the resurrection of the "Christ" in us, our higher spiritual self, from burial in our "lower nature".'
4. A delightful way of expressing the new relationship.

CHAPTER SIX

The parables

If there is one thing all of us recall about Jesus it is that he was a storyteller, a teller of tales called 'parables'. 'Listen ye. A sower went forth to sow his seed ....' His voice calls to us across the centuries from the shore of ancient Galilee. We join that listening crowd. A silence falls. 'He that hath ears to hear, let him hear ....' In the stillness, the seed is instilled, the word is sown.

The Sufis have always been great storytellers and have produced many wonderful tales through which to transmit their message. These tales they call 'teaching stories'. They are subtle creations, reaching to and resonating at different levels of our consciousness. In this way they change and develop us, though they can only have their full effect when used as an organic part of a total teaching situation. They require, say the Sufis, certain conditions for their proper operation. These include 'the time, the place, and the people'.

Nothing more clearly identifies Jesus of Nazareth as an exponent of the Sufi Way than his use of parables. And so it is not surprising that tales by and about Jesus have long been in use in and continue to be used in Sufi circles. Much of this material is, as one might expect, not recorded in the New Testament. Some, however, has fortunately been preserved in the New Testament Apocrypha, notably the extraordinary 'Hymn of the Pearl'. This is strikingly similar to the Sufi tale 'The King's Son', which can be found in Idries Shah's *Tales of the Dervishes* (see page 108).

If the objective of the School of Jesus was entry into the Kingdom of Heaven, then the parables can be regarded as 'keys' to the Kingdom, but keys that could only be 'turned' in the totality of the teaching. Many of the parables do, of course, refer to the kingdom quite explicitly, beginning for example 'The kingdom of heaven is like a mustard seed' or 'The kingdom is like leaven'. These are not 'comparisons', but immediate and active symbolic agents of transformation which in some mysterious way emit an impulse which carries you *towards* the kingdom.

The parable is thus a symbolic organism spiritually imbued with something of the texture of the kingdom itself. It is a living ladder, let down from above, drawing us up. The parable of the mustard seed *is* the mustard seed. It makes us grow through its intrinsic power of growth. And the parable of the leaven (hidden in the dough) is that very leaven.

Thomas Merton grasped something of this action when he said:

> The true symbol does not merely point to something else. It contains in itself a 'something' which awakens our consciousness to an awareness of the inner meaning of life and of reality itself.

And Amos Wilder perceptively observes: 'Parables are potent—potent words. They offer 'revelatory shocks'. They are not comparisons with, but bearers of reality.'

Parables irrupt from another dimension, connecting us with their source, raising us towards their plane of origin. They are inter-dimensional being-transmission. They transform and transport. And so they are miracles, as miracles are parables.

To benefit from them we must receive them. They are 'the harvest of a quiet ear'—the receptive inner ear, the ear that can hear,[1] as the parable of the Sower informs us. For this first parable delivered by Jesus is a parable about how to learn from parables—an introduction to the art of listening. 'And he said unto them, "Know ye not this parable? And how then will ye know all parables?"'

'The Sower' is about levels of reception, and what prevents it reaching its deepest level.[2] A parable is a deep-speech event issuing from the very being of its speaker, the deep-man Jesus. Such communication requires a certain alignment or attunement between transmitter and receiver, an inner alertness which Jesus describes as 'hearing ability'. This faculty is so important that the saying 'He that hath ears to hear, let him hear' is constantly repeated through the New Testament—seventeen times in all. In one of the Oxyrhynchus sayings Jesus puts it like this: 'Thou hearest with one ear. But the other ear thou hast closed [the inner ear].' The Sower is thus concerned with the identification of different degrees of hearing and closure.

> And he said unto them, Hearken:
> A sower went forth to sow his seed:
> and as he sowed, some fell by the wayside;
> and the fowls of the air came and devoured it.
> And some fell upon stony ground,[3]
> where it had not much earth;
> and immediately it sprang up,
> because it had no depth of earth.
>
> But when the sun was up
> it was scorched; and because it had no root,
> it withered away.
> And some fell among thorns,

and the thorns grew up,
and choked it.

And other fell on good ground
and brought forth fruit,
some thirty,
some sixty,
and some an hundredfold.

He that hath ears to hear—
let him hear.

I have written the parable as poetry because it is a special kind of 'teaching poem' which Sufi masters use to communicate a mystical message. Rumi, Saadi, Hafiz and Omar Khayyam were all masters of this art. As indeed was Idries Shah—whose poetry is in his prose.

We will never know what that gathering by Galilee really heard as Jesus delivered his parable-poems:[4] the power, the pauses, the rhythms and resonance of the master's telling. Yet in the written form something strangely persists. We still hear the distinct tones of that individual voice. 'Hearken', it says— 'hearken with your heart.'

'The sower soweth the word', he tells us, which is 'the word of the kingdom'. But soils vary as mediums of growth, according to their depth and quality. Their receptive and sustaining power are different. The hard soil of the roadway does not receive the seed at all—cannot even 'register' the word. No germination can occur there. In the shallow soil of the stony ground proper rooting is impossible. The roots do not grow deep enough. 'These are they who have no root in themselves.' Says Jesus. A telling phrase if ever there was one. Such people, it seems, have lost contact with the very root of their being.

He continues: 'And these are they which are sown among thorns: such as hear the word, and the cares of this world, and the deceitfulness of riches, choke the word and it becometh unfruitful.'

The Sufi constantly draws attention to the many things that besiege and beset the soul, that becloud its vision, and cause it to forget. The 'world' in Sufi parlance is all that inveigles and weighs down the self, and wastes its potential. In the parable of the Prodigal Son we are told that 'he took his journey into a far country, and there *wasted his substance.'*[5]

And finally, says Jesus: 'But that on the good ground are they, which in an honest and good heart, having heard the word, keep it, and bring forth fruit with patience.'

These are the open-hearted who, uncluttered and unencumbered by the various bonds and blockages which prevent true hearing, hear and hold the word, receive it and retain it.

Jesus here refers to the need for an 'honest' heart. The honesty he is talking about is, according to Sufis, a special quality radiating from the inner self, which is connected with sincerity. It must be cultivated and allowed to shine through. In turn, spiritual honesty of this kind enables the soul itself to grow. From the Sufi point of view honesty is not so much a virtue as an art, to reveal and give access to the inner self, enabling it to come into operation. In his very next parable, delivered directly after 'The Sower', Jesus says: 'Is a candle brought to be put under a bushel?'

Jesus, in common with all Sufis, also stresses the importance of patience as a necessary aspect of 'the good ground' that will 'bring forth fruit'. Patience enables one to learn, to perceive. It provides correct alignment with the Teaching. Impatience immediately places you out of contact with it, and yourself. As he said: 'Possess your soul in patience.' In other words, impatience dispossesses you of it.

Edgar Cayce once remarked that patience was a dimension. 'There are three dimensions,' he said, 'Time, Space and Patience.' A valuable insight.

I am reminded of this poem.

The Planet Patience

Come with me to the Planet Patience,
Come with me there;
And we will see more surely,
In its clear air.
There on its waiting waters
A Lily lies,
And from the Plains of Patience,
The Eternal Mountains rise.

The last two lines of the poem appear to tell us that eternity can only be perceived *through* patience.

The parable of 'The Sower' is thus concerned with the cultivation of a certain 'inner space' within one, a 'clearing' within which the inner consciousness can grow. In his comment on the parable the master points out that patience and honesty are indispensable instruments for this process. In his Parable of Wisdom, recorded and preserved for us by the great Sufi, Al Ghazali,[6] Jesus calls attention to another essential learning quality:

The Parable of Wisdom

Jesus asked, 'That which you sow, where does it grow?' The people answered, 'In good ground.'

He continued, 'In the same way Wisdom does not grow in the heart unless it is a good soil for it. The harvest does not grow on the mountain but in the plains. Wisdom grows too in the hearts of the lowly.'

In this beautiful parable Jesus, like other great teachers, stresses the absolute necessity of humility for the seeker of wisdom. Note that he is not praising it as a virtue, but, like all Sufis, explaining that it is essential to the learning process, to the growth of understanding. Humility attunes one to the reception of the Teaching. It is, as Sufis say 'a means of travel'. But it must be the right kind of humility. This is something one actually learns, and acquires as one follows the Way. Its distortion is self-abasement.

So the opposite of humility—pride—is not criticised by the Sufis as a 'vice' but simply as something that puts you 'in a vice', locks you in! It incapacitates—disables from learning. Pride therefore does not necessarily 'come before a fall'. It prevents a climb.

Humility and honesty are thus related. If one is really honest—honest to oneself—humility automatically appears. It is in fact one's natural, normal state, obscured by the abnormality of false pride (I am admitting by implication that there is such a thing as 'real' pride). But honesty and humility depend in part on the development of one's consciousness and concomitant self-knowledge. Then one knows one has much less to be proud about than one imagines! Under the searchlight of consciousness the clouds of concealed conceit are dispelled, and lo and behold—one *is* humble after all!

'Humility is directly concerned with the quest for Absolute Truth' says Idries Shah. While an earlier teacher said: 'It is easier for a camel to pass through the eye of a needle than for a rich man to enter the kingdom of heaven.' Here 'rich' does not refer to worldly wealth as usually understood, but the burden and blockage of being too full of oneself, too puffed up with pride to enter 'the strait gate' of the kingdom. When Jesus said this, his audience would know that the Eye of a Needle was a small low entrance in the city wall of Jerusalem, originally made by Moses himself so that his people would be forced to stoop as they used it—and be thus reminded of the need for humility. To expand you must first contract.

The wise man increases by decreasing.

(*Tao Te Ching*)

When thou art bidden, go and sit down in the lowest room ....

For whosoever exalteth himself shall be abased; and he that humbleth himself shall be exalted.

(Luke 14.11)

He that hath not humbled himself in his heart Cannot ascend unto His holy hill

(Psalm 24.3)

Humility is a means of travel

(Sufi saying)

The Parable of the Seed growing Secretly

The parable of Wisdom explicitly communicates the great truth that wisdom is something that *grows*. 'Wisdom grows in the hearts of the lowly' says Jesus. It grows as a plant grows, organically. It is not acquired, but assimilated—as a plant absorbs sunlight. One grows in wisdom as one grows *into* Wisdom. For it is all around and within us. Humility exposes one to this Light, which transforms one, and then enables one to participate in it, and with it.

But one must accept that the nature of this process is subtle and invisible. It cannot be understood until understanding itself develops. The parable which follows that of the Sower conveys this truth:

> And he said:
> So is the kingdom of God
> as if a man should cast seed
> into the ground,
> and should sleep and rise
> night and day,
> and the seed should spring,
> and grow up,
> he knoweth not how.

Inner growth is bound to be largely a mysterious process. What else could one expect of a movement from one level of consciousness to another, higher level? Jesus, like all Sufis, is stressing that the seeker should *allow* himself to be taught, to receive the teaching, without imposing his own preconceptions of what it might be, upon it. In order to know he must learn to unknow.

Jesus then delivers the Parable of the Mustard Seed.

> The kingdom of heaven is like to
> a grain of mustard seed
> which a man took, and sowed in his field:
> which indeed is the least of all seeds:
> but when it is grown
> it is the greatest among herbs,
> and becometh a tree—
> so that the birds of the air come
> and lodge in the branches thereof.

I suggest that Jesus presented this and other parables with his very *being*. By bringing his being into communication with the inner being of those whom he was addressing, by projecting his spiritual power upon them, he activated the 'mustard seed' within his hearers and caused it to grow. This is called 'heart to heart communication' by the Sufis. Jesus refers to it as the flowing of 'living water'. Without it spiritual seeds won't grow.

It is interesting to read in juxtaposition to this parable the following instructions for transmutation by the Chinese alchemist, Lu Tsu:

> I must diligently plant my own field. There is within it a
> spiritual germ that may live a thousand years. Its flower
> is like yellow gold. Its bud is not large, but its seeds are
> round and like unto a spotless gem. Its growth depends
> upon the soil of the central palace, but its irrigation must
> proceed from a higher fountain.

HEAVEN

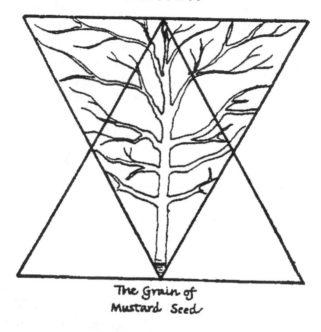

The Grain of
Mustard Seed

EARTH

This beautifully expresses the growth of the inner spiritual
tree from the temporal to the eternal. It is the concept of
Maurice Nicoll in *The Mark*.

Translated into Sufi terms by a contemporary master this
reads:

Man must develop by his own effort towards growth of an
evolutionary nature, stabilising his consciousness. He has
within him an essence, initially tiny, shining, precious.
Development depends upon man, but must start through
a teacher. When the mind is cultivated[7] correctly and suit-
ably, the consciousness is translated to a sublime plane.

We are talking, then, of the potential development of the essence, the inner consciousness. The mustard seed is 'the least of all seeds' because from one point of view it has no 'size' at all, nor does it exist in place. It is qualitative rather than quantitative, residing where time meets eternity.[8]

The growth of the mustard plant takes place entirely within an invisible inner dimension. It rises, from its roots in the 'earth', to its branches, breaking the planes, into the 'air'. It is really the Tree of Wisdom—so great and tall that its leaves wave in heaven.

'The birds of the air' that then 'come and lodge in the branches' are the impulses of illumination that according to the Sufi come from the invisible world and fly to the heart which has been awakened.

After the plant parables, each complementing the others, Jesus tells the Parable of the Leaven:

> Another parable spake he unto them:
>> the kingdom of heaven
>> is like leaven
>> which a woman took
>> and hid in three measures of meal,
>> till the whole was leavened.
>
> (Matthew 13.33)

As one participates in this parable of process one senses the inner working of a spiritual leaven that permeates and penetrates all that comes into contact with it—till the whole is raised. It is a total operation of suffusion and interfusion. It is about transformation from within; what Sufis call 'irradiation'. It is about a sea change into something rich and strange.

Yet, as has already been said, parables are not in reality 'about' anything, They *are* something. They have to be experienced in themselves. Their meaning is in their movement—their inner movement. What do a bird's wings 'mean'?

So at the time of delivery from the master, the leaven entered and 'raised' the very hearts of the hearers.

I am not however suggesting all Jesus' parables are teaching stories. Some, like the Prodigal Son, undoubtedly are. Many however would be better described as teaching poems, luminous with a single living image, a soul-creating metaphor. Such symbolic organisms, while similar in effect, and related to, the Sufic tale, are not necessarily the fully developed artefact that the teaching story proper usually is.

Again, to harvest their full effect, their full yield, one would have had to have been a student in the actual School of Jesus. Or to make contact with a genuine contemporary Sufi school.

Finally, it is interesting to hear the response of a Christian priest to a recent collection of authentic Suf teaching stories. The Reverend Sidney Spencer has this to say:

> The meaning of these stories is often highly enigmatic. It does not by any means lie on the surface. The teaching story springs from, and makes its appeal to, the inner and greater self that lies, as the Sufis (like all mystics) maintain, beyond the normal and superficial self, which is blind to its own deeper being. The stories are calculated to bring into play, perhaps by their strangeness and unexpectedness, the forces of the hidden life.

This is a significant act of spiritual recognition, transcending the closed paradigm of religious orthodoxy.

How then should one approach these tales? I would suggest with calm receptivity to whatever there *is* to be received. Without puzzling over them, without seeking to impose interpretations upon or wrest interpretations from them. Simply read them and see what they say. As Pamela Travers wisely advises, 'Let the tale tell *you* what it means'.

And if the meaning doesn't immediately manifest—don't worry. Simply absorb them, and they will act upon you at a deeper level. Like the seed growing secretly in Jesus's parable.

Here is a teaching story in current use. It is recorded by Idries Shah in *Tales of the Devishes*.

Strike on this spot

Dhun-Nun the Egyptian explained graphically in a parable how he extracted knowledge concealed in Pharaonic insciriptions.

There was a statue with pointing finger, upon which was inscribed: 'Strike on this spot for treasure'. Its origin was unknown, but generations of people had hammered the place marked by the sign. Because it was made of the hardest stone, little impression was made on it, and the meaning remained cryptic.

Dhun-Nun, wrapped in contemplation of the statue, one day exactly at midday observed that the *shadow* of the pointing finger, unnoticed for centuries, followed a line in the paving beneath the statue.

Marking the place he obtained the necessary instruments and prised up by chisel-blows the flagstone, which proved to be the trapdoor in the roof of a subterranean cave which contained strange articles of a workmanship which enabled him to deduce the science of their manufacture, long since lost, and hence to acquire the treasures and those of a more formal kind which accompanied them.

Almost the same story is told by Pope Sylvester II, who brought 'Arabian' learning, including mathematics, from Seville in Spain in the tenth century.

Reputedly a magician because of his technical attainments, Gerbert (as he was originally called) 'lodged with a philosopher of the Saracen sect'. It was almost certainly here that he learned of this Sufi tale.

It is said to have been passed on by the Caliph Abu-Bakr, who died in 634.

Notes

1. 'O hear ye this, all ye people: ponder it with your ears. I will incline mine ear to the parable: and shew my dark speech upon the harp.' (Psalm 49). 'And we set forth these parables for man that he may reflect.' (The Koran. Sura Hashr, 21).

2. 'It is the heart of man that makes its possessor hear or not hear.' (*Ptahhotep* of Egypt, 2800 BC). Jesus concurs with the Egyptian sage that to be hard of heart means to be hard of hearing when he says (Matthew 13.15): 'For this people's heart is waxed gross, and their ears are dull of hearing ...'. And 'Perceive ye not, neither do ye understand? Have ye your heart yet hardened?' (Mark 8.17, 18).

   In this connection Sufis use as technical terms 'The film and the veil' to refer to 'Whatever covers the mirror of the Heart with rust and dulls the eye of insight, spreading over the face of its mirror' (Al-Qashani). The 'heart' is the Sufi term for the higher perceptive faculty of humankind, intuitive in nature, which must be purified and developed.

3. The Greek word *petrodes* actually means 'shallow soil, with underlying rocks'.

4. 'In a hidden way and in a mystery, carrying the symbolic meaning, such things are said into the ear.' (Clement of Alexandria—*Stromateis* VI. 124).

5. That is, wasted *himself*—as most of us do.

6. In his *Ihya al-Olum'*.

7. In the version of this parable in the Gospel of Thomas (hajion 20) the field is significantly described as 'tilled' or cultivated.

8. 'He hath set eternity in the *heart* of man.' (Ecclesiastes III. 11).

   'If you make a small circle, as small as a little grain, or Kernel of seed, there is the whole birth of the Eternal Nature.' (Jacob Boehme—*Mysterium Magnum*).

CHAPTER SEVEN

The sayings

Verily, verily I say unto you: If a man *keep*[1] my sayings, he shall never see death' says Jesus (John 8.51). And the Gospel of Thomas begins:

> These are the secret words which the living Jesus spoke and Didymus Judas Thomas wrote. And he said: 'Whoever finds the meaning of these words will not taste death.'

Sufi masters have long used certain 'sayings' as an integral aspect of their teaching, and Jesus was an able exponent of this traditional technique. Like the parables, these teaching-sayings are concentrated, multi-dimensional entities which, when properly pondered and contemplated, will act constructively upon the consciousness and affect the very texture of one's being.

It is now well established that a collection of sayings and parables is the underlying common core of the Gospels. This was the original primal material around which the Gospel writers composed their various texts. These frames consisted of biographies of Jesus seen from and interpreted through the doctrinal viewpoint and beliefs of the early Church. The 'overlay' made it difficult to discern and identify the original teaching. As Harnack observed: 'The gospel *of* Jesus became the gospel *about* Jesus.' And thus it came about that he who lived to teach us 'died to save us'!

It is impossible to know whether there were one or several collections of these sayings and parables, but it is certain that the corpus was partly oral and partly written. Valuable evidence regarding the existence of an oral tradition, and also the respect in which it was held, comes from Papias, who was the bishop of Hierapolis in Phrygia early in the second century. Papias wrote a five-volume treatise entitled *Lxpositions of the Oracles of the Lord*, a translation of the Greek *Logion Kyriakon Exegesis*. 'Oracles' meant 'sayings'. Very unfortunately this work has been almost entirely lost. Only a few fragments remain, in the form of quotations preserved in *Historia Ecclesia* by Eusebius, the Church historian. The object of the work seems to have been to throw light on the Gospels with the help of oral traditions which Papias had been able to collect from those who had come into direct contact with any of the inner group of twelve disciples, and occasionally surviving members of this group whom he had actually met himself.

> If ever any one came who had been a follower of the Elders, I would enquire as to the discourses of the Elders, what was said by Andrew, or what by Peter, or what by Philip, or what by Thomas or James, or what by John or Matthew, or any other of the disciples of the Lord; and the things which Aristion and the elder John,[2] the disciples of the Lord say. For I did not think that I could get so much profit from the contents of books as from the utterances of a living and abiding voice.

We may well wonder what we have lost! The reference to an unknown disciple, Aristion, is interesting. Nothing more is known of him—except that in the margin of an Armenian manuscript of the Gospels dated 986, discovered by F. C. Conybeare in 1891, is a statement attributing Mark 16.9–20 (the final verses of this gospel) to the 'Elder Aristion'.

Papias' book was extant much later than is commonly supposed. A volume described as *The Book of Papias*, the Book of the Words of the Lord is known to have been in the Church of Nîmes about 1218. And even later, in the 15th century, there appears to have been a copy in England, for John Boston, a monk and bibliographer of Bury, includes 'Papias of Hierapolis' in his list of writers whose works he had seen in monastic libraries.

But returning to our theme of 'the Sayings tradition', another statement of Papias preserved by Eusebius is of considerable significance. Discussing the composition of the Gospels he says: 'The elder John used to say, Mark having become Peter's interpreter, wrote accurately all that he remembered, though he did not record in order that which was said or done by Jesus. For he neither heard the Lord nor followed him ....' Then he makes the statement: 'Matthew composed the oracles in Hebrew, and every one interpreted them as he could.'

Now this is extremely important information from a reliable near-contemporary source that the first Gospel of Matthew was none other than a book of sayings and parables, 'oracles'—and in Hebrew. The Gospel of Matthew we have received is presented as a biographical narrative and is believed, like all the Gospels in the New Testament, to have been written in Greek. In view of Papias' testimony this is not the original Matthew but an altered and different document, though containing whatever material from the earlier book that the 'author' chose to include. It also means that, contrary to currently fashionable scholarly opinion, Matthew, the real Matthew, and not Mark, was the first Gospel—as early Christians unanimously believed. Which was why they arranged the four gospels in the order: Matthew, Mark, Luke, and John (as they explained).

It is now agreed by most scholars that the Gospels of Matthew and of Luke as we find them in the New Testament were based on two sources: Mark, which was written earlier, and also another, unidentified source tentatively called 'Q', which appears to have been a collection of Sayings by Jesus. It has sometimes been called 'the unknown Gospel'.

It is here suggested that 'Q' was none other than this original ur-Matthew itself, the book of 'oracles' mentioned by Papias— later to be elaborated by another writer, with the help of a biographical narrative from Mark, into the Matthew we have been presented with.

Further evidence on this matter comes from Epiphanius. He tells us that the group of early Christians known as the Nazarenes and that called the Ebionites both used a Gospel of Matthew in Hebrew. This corroborates Papias—whom scholars yet choose to ignore. Could this be the real meaning of 'ignorant'?

What then was that lost gospel of Matthew like? Since December 1945 we have been in the very fortunate position of being able to answer that question. For the *Gospel of Thomas*, discovered with the forty-eight other texts in the sands of Egypt near Nag Hammadi at that date, must surely be a work of this 'genre'. Here we have a collection of oral teachings of Jesus, sayings and parables, both known and unknown, together with interesting variants of familiar ones. It is very probable that these 'sayings' of Thomas were like the 'oracles' of Matthew and other early Christian teaching texts that have been lost.

The Gospel of Thomas is simply and wholly concerned with the presentation of teaching statements by Jesus, introduced every time with the words 'Jesus said'. There is no narrative. There is no mention of his birth, the external incidents of his life, the miracles, nor of his 'death'. There are no 'apocalyptic' statements, nor any mention of a 'second coming'. The gospel is in no way concerned with events in time. It is concerned solely with entry into eternity or eternal life. 'Whoever finds the meaning of these words will not taste death.' Eternal is of course a qualitative concept. It refers to intensity rather than extensity, being rather than surviving, consciousness rather than continuity. Eternal life is thus synonymous with the kingdom of heaven. 'Be above time', says Jesus to his disciples in the *Gospel of Mary* (discovered in Akhmim, Egypt in 1896), while a later Sufi, Samarkandi Amini, has exhorted: 'Pass from time and place, to timelessness and placelessness—to the other world. There is our origin.'

The *Gospel of Thomas* is in fact closely concerned with the relationship between man and the Origin: his coming from, his connection with, and his possible return to it.

> Jesus said: Blessed are the solitary and elect
> for you shall find the kingdom;
> because you come from it
> you shall go there again.
> Jesus said: If they say to you
> 'From where have you originated?'
> say to them: 'We have come from the Light,
> where the Light has originated through itself.'
> If they say to you: 'Who are you?'
> say 'We are His sons and daughters,
> the elect of the Living Father.'
> If they ask you:
> 'What is the sign of your Father in you?',
> say to them:
> 'It is a movement and a rest'.

We learn that the higher life is one of spiritual action, perfectly poised in peace.

The 'solitary' are those who can stand single and sole, wholly alone in their true inner selves, unbesieged and unpolluted by all that is not themselves. They have realised their true identity.

One of the Sufi arts is the practice of 'Solitude in company'. It is in fact one of the ten 'rules' of the Naqshbandi Order.

It is clear both from its introduction ('These are the secret words which the living Jesus spoke') and from its content that we are dealing with an esoteric document. The fact that some of this material is also to be found in variant form in the well-known Gospels merely indicates that this is esoteric too, despite the 'veil of familiarity' that obscures us to this truth. To this extent we can agree with the observation of P. D. Ouspensky that 'esotericism occupies a very important place in Christian teaching and in the New Testament if these are properly understood'. Though he failed to add that they can only properly be understood through esotericism itself. It is the esoteric current that gives them life, that carries us to their inner meaning. For esotericism is known by means of itself, which implies real involvement, in the real work, of a real school.

We will now look at a number of other sayings from the 114 sayings and parables recorded in the Gospel of Thomas, noting where possible their affinity with sayings from the Sufi tradition.

To begin with, an interaction significantly setting the tone, and highlighting the kind of approach Jesus wishes to inculcate in his students:

> Thomas said to him: Master, my mouth will not at all be capable of saying whom thou art like.
>
> Jesus said: I am not thy Master, because thou hast drunk from the bubbling spring which I have merely meted out.

Here Jesus, in true Sufi style, deflects the disciple's attention from himself to the Teaching. As Rumi puts it: 'Do not look at my outward shape, but take what is in my hand.'

> There are many around the well
> but nobody in the well.

This obviously esoteric saying is also recorded by Origen, the third century scholar and Christian thinker, in his work *Contra Celsus*, in the form of a question which he says Jesus used often to ask: 'Why are there so many about the well—and no-one *in* the well?'

The 'well' is a perennial symbol of the Sufis, occurring frequently in their teaching material, as in: 'Whoever has not first dug a well should not steal a minaret.'

And one recalls the proverb: 'Truth lies at the bottom of a well'.

There is also the proverb of inner meaning in the Book of Proverbs (v.15) of the Old Testament:

> Drink waters out of thine own cistern, and
> running waters out of thine own well.

Another esoteric saying by Jesus in the *Gospel of Thomas* is: 'Become passers by'. He is here communicating a state of detachment, of non-identification with worldly things, which is a necessary aspect of spiritual development. Note that one has to *become* this. It is an achievement as a result of guided work on oneself. It, of course, in no way implies moral indifference. This saying, like many other sayings of Jesus, is probably what the Sufis call a 'meditation-theme'—to be dwelt on inwardly for its transformative power. The following better-known saying in Matthew (8.20) should perhaps be approached in the same way:

> The foxes have holes, and the birds of the air have
> nests; but the son of man hath no where to lay his head.

Of profound interest is the following Saying (84) of the *Gospel of Thomas*:

> Jesus said:
>> When you see your likeness, you rejoice.
>> But when you see your images which
>> came into existence before you,
>> which neither die nor are manifested,
>> how much will you bear!

The master is here referring to the need to rediscover and uncover one's true inner self, the eternal essence that must emerge and evolve. This is the self that is to be known in the exhortation 'Know thyself'. This is the 'the light that is hidden under a bushel.'

Hence Jesus said (Saying 19):

> 'Blessed is he who is as he was before he
> came into being.'

The great Sufi, Dhun-Nun the Egyptian, known as 'Lord of the Fish', instructed: 'Be as you were, where you were, before you were.' And the Sufi master Hakim Sanai of Afghanistan tells us:

> The human's progress is like that of one who has
> been given a sealed book, written before he was born.
> He carries it inside himself until he 'dies'.
> While man is subject to the movement of Time, he
> does not know the contents of that sealed book.

In another saying in the *Gospel of Thomas*, Jesus says:

> You have five trees in Paradise
> which are unmoved in summer or winter

and their leaves do not fall.
Whoever knows them
shall not taste death.

This is the esoteric doctrine that the soul has five senses of its own. These are the human inner faculties that have to be gradually alerted for the attainment of full Consciousness. The Sufis call them the Five Subtleties (*Lataif-i-Khamsa*). Idries Shah gives us information on this subject in *A Perfumed Scorpion*, a valuable introduction to the nature of Sufi education. However, the classic Sufi text on the inner faculties is *The Sacred Knowledge of the Higher Functions of the Mind*, by the great teacher Shah Waliullah of Delhi. According to this authority, through the purification and development of these faculties 'a man is able to be present in the heavenly fold of the world to come.' That is, while still on earth.

We will now turn to a little-known and much-neglected source of sayings by Jesus—the considerable corpus of material preserved in the Middle East in Islamic countries, and recorded by Al Ghazali and other Sufis.

How did such traditions find their way to these areas? The answer is that from the first century onwards there were Christian missions to the East as well as to the West. Some of the Arab tribes were Christianised hundreds of years before Islam arrived, and there were a number of Christian monasteries in Arabia at the time of Mohammed. In fact, the first man to recognise Mohammed as a new prophet and to give him confidence in his summons was his cousin Waraqa ibn Naufal, a learned Christian.

Before long, however, the whole of Arabia was Islamicised, or 'converted to Islam', if one prefers. As the conquests extended beyond the bounds of Arabia the Moslems came into contact with other Christian communities. Christians were given the alternative of either accepting Islam or paying tribute—and while many adopted the new religion, just as many retained their Christianity. The latter were thereafter, according to good historical evidence, treated with tolerance and fairness. It is therefore easy to see how a body of oral and written material connected with Jesus should have survived *within* the Islamic domain, through both the converted and the unconverted.

It is also important to bear in mind in this regard that Jesus is held in the highest honour and esteem in Islam. The Qur'an makes it clear that, like Mohammed, he was both a prophet and a Messenger (Rasul) and taught people to surrender to God— the central concept and meaning of 'Islam'. Jesus is described as 'an eminent one in this world and the next' and as 'One of those brought near to God'. In Chapter 57 comes the following affirmation:

> We formerly sent Noah and Abraham, appointed them as prophets, and the Book to be in their posterity. In their footsteps we caused Jesus to follow, and We gave him the Gospel containing guidance and light.

Thus Jesus's mandate from on High is made clear to every Moslem. This, in turn, explains why so many sayings and parables by him, and stories about him, were so valued, and preserved. The Sufis, of course, particularly valued them for their Sufic content and therefore took a special interest in their survival. A number of these sayings are recorded in the

New Testament. But many are not. Here is a selection from the latter category:

> The world is merely a bridge: pass over it, but don't build your dwelling upon it.

This appears as an inscription in Arabic upon the gateway of the mosque in the ruined city of Fateh-pur-Sikri, eleven miles south of Delhi, near Agra, built by the Moghul emperor Akbar in the 16th century. I remember being taken there as a child of about nine, and our guide, a learned Moslem, pointing it out and translating it for us.

> Be in the midst, yet walk on one side.

The Nazarene master, at his most quintessential, expresses the Sufi aim: 'Be in the world, but not of the world.' The saying is recorded by the Sufi teacher Al-Ghazali (known in the West as the great mediaeval philosopher Algazel), in his *Ihya al-olum ad Din*, which contains a considerable number of Jesus' sayings and parables.

> Remember cotton when it is put over your eyes.

This saying was quoted by the Sufi master of the ninth century, Maaruf Karkhi. The subject is, of course, the need for awareness of obstacles to inner perception. We are veiled from our selves by our ourselves, say the Sufis. 'You yourself are under your own veil' (Hafiz).

Sufian al Thauri used to say: 'A man said to Jesus (Blessing and peace be upon him!) "Give me some advice." He replied, "Consider where your bread comes from."

The master here provides a contemplation-theme for orientation towards the origins of things. 'The visible is a bridge to the Invisible', as Sufis say.

Rumi says in his *Diwan of Shams of Tabriz*.

> Every form you see has its essence in the Placeless.
> If the form goes, no matter, for its origin is everlasting ....

* * *

> Verily you will obtain what you like only by your patience
> with what you dislike.

This saying is recorded by Al-Ghazali in his great *Revival of the Spiritual Art*. There is a Sufi saying: 'Patience is bitter—but bears a sweet fruit.' Al-Ghazali says:

> Jesus (God bless him and grant him peace!) said:
> 'The friends of God are they who look into the inner
> things of the world when men look at its outward things,
> and at its hereafter when men look at its present.'

> God revealed to Jesus:
> 'Keep yourself hungry, that you may see Me; and be
> detached, that you may be joined to Me.'
> —A tradition recorded by Razi in his *Mersad al-ebad*.

> Jesus said: 'Devote yourselves to obtaining that which
> fire cannot burn.' 'And what is that', asked the disciples.
> 'Virtue', he replied'
> —Al-Ghazali, in his *Revival*.

> It is said that the sole worldly possession of Jesus was
> a cup from which he drank water. One day he happened
> to see a man drinking water from his cupped hand.
> Thenceforth he did without his cup, declaring:
> 'Till now I was unaware that God had bestowed a cup
> upon me.'
> —Quoted by the Sufi, Ansari—a teaching-incident.

'Blessed is he who stores away his tongue, and whose house contains him.'

—Related on the authority of Salim, son of Abu al Ja'd.

Jesus, among other things, calls attention to our lack of presence in ourselves. How often is one really 'at home'?—The need for self-possession.

'Verily I say unto you, he who has not been born twice will not see the kingdom of heaven and the earth. By God, verily we are of those who have been born twice. The first birth is the birth of nature, and the second birth is the birth of the spirit in the heaven of knowledge.'

—Recorded by Al-Ghazali.

And finally:

Jesus said: When you make the two one, you shall become sons of Man.

In this saying Jesus expresses the same truth as the Sufi, Hakim Sansai in his classic *The Walled Garden*: 'The pure man unites two in one.'

I hesitate to comment on this mysterious saying. But it may mean the necessary union of the outer and inner self.

Finally here are a number of Jesus' sayings preserved from various sources, some known, some unknown which are provided for their intrinsic value and interest:

Further sayings of Jesus, recorded by Al Ghazali, Thalabi and others

It is related that a pig passed by Jesus (peace be upon him!)

and he said, 'Pass in peace.' Then someone said, 'O man of God, do you say this to a pig?' He replied, 'I dislike accustoming my tongue to evil.'

Jesus said, 'You say that I have been able to raise the dead, and that is true. But mark well that I was unable to cure the foolishness of fools.'

It is related on the authority of Jesus (Peace be upon him!) 'Silence is the beginning of worship.'

Jesus said: 'If a man send away a beggar empty from his house, the angels will not visit that house for seven nights.'

Jesus (Peace be upon him!) said: 'Blessed is he who abandons a present desire for a distant promise he has not seen.'

The Devil said to Jesus, 'Say there is no God but God.' Jesus answered, 'That is true, but I shall not repeat it after you!'

It has reached us that Jesus, son of Mary, (Peace be upon him!) said, 'Verily I say unto you, do not be like a sieve from which the good flour goes out and in which the siftings remain.'

Jesus used to say 'He who does not collect, scatters himself'.

Jesus passed an afflicted man and treated him kindly and said: 'O God, I beseech Thee to heal him!' Then God (Exalted is He) revealed to him,

'How can I heal him from that with which I am healing him?'

One day Jesus was lying with a stone beneath his head, as a pillow. The Devil passed by, and called out, 'Jesus, that stone shows your dependence upon things of this world!' Jesus took up the stone and threw it at him, crying, 'Take it, and the world with it!'

Jesus (Peace be upon him!) said, 'Seek a great amount of what fire cannot consume.' Someone said, 'And what is that?' He said, 'Kindness.'

Notes

1. To 'keep' a saying seems to imply to 'make it one's own, *organically* part of one.'
2. Note the final verse of John's Gospel: 'And there are also many other things which Jesus did, the which, if they should be written every one, I suppose that even the world itself could not contain the books that should be written. Amen.' (John 21:25).
3. 'Love thy neighbour as thyself.' (Luke 10.27).

CHAPTER EIGHT

Jesus and the animals

It is often alleged or assumed that there is no clear reference to the way man should relate to the animals in the teaching of Jesus, beyond the well-known saying about sparrows at Luke 12.6: 'Not one of them is forgotten before God.' Even if that were true, not only does this statement contain profound implications for the matter in itself—but surely his whole message of compassion must be taken to include compassion for all our fellow creatures. I suspect that many who call themselves Christians have not yet really reflected on this question, leaving it to others to articulate the ethics involved. Sadly, the Church has shown little concern in the matter.

But if we take into account all the evidence that is available, Jesus' message is clear. It is that to be human is to be human to animals. Which surely should come as no surprise!

In 1881 an ancient Aramaic Gospel was discovered by the scholar and explorer the Reverend J.G.R. Ousley in a Tibetan *gompa* (monastery). The text describes, among other things, how one day Jesus entered a small village where he found a kitten which was not cared for. Jesus picked her up and put her inside his garment. He gave food and drink to the little cat, who was hungry. Some of the villagers expressed surprise that he should show such care for so insignificant a creature. Jesus said:

> Verily, these are your fellow creatures of the great household of the Eternal Being. They are indeed thy brethren and sisters, and have the same breath of life in Eternal God, and are breathing the same spirit.

Ernest Scott, author of that great study of the Magnum Opus in history, *The People of the Secret*, in which he shows considerable knowledge of Sufic activity, offers this insight:

> Najmuddin Kubra and St Francis were making a point that the animal world and not just the human world had a place in the Great Work which would later be called evolution. I wonder if Robert Burns, the Scots poet, had caught a whiff of it when, talking to a mouse, he said:

> > I'm truly sorry man's dominion
> > Has broken Nature's social union
> > That justifies that ill opinion
> > That makes thee start at me
> > Thy poor Earth-born companion
> > And fellow mortal!

I'm grateful to both these fine men of Scotland for alerting us to this matter. Doubtless the 'dominion' which Robbie

Burns refers to is that mentioned in Genesis 1.28, where God supposedly puts humanity over the animals. I think he would not be altogether surprised to learn that the original Hebrew word which has been mistranslated into English as 'dominion' actually means 'stewardship'—a rather different concept. A steward, I understand, is someone entrusted with taking *care* of 'property' for someone else, the real owner.

And now we come to a little-known incident in the life of Jesus which, though not esoteric in its implications, is included here for its message for a time when the bond of compassion that should unite us to our lesser fellow creatures is being so wilfully ignored.

'It happened that the Lord went forth from the city and walked with his disciples over the mountains. And they came to a mountain, and the road which led to it was steep. There they found a man with a sumptermule. But the animal had fallen, for the burden was too heavy, and he beat it that it bled. And Jesus came to him and said, 'Man, why dost thou beat thine animal? Seest thou not that it is too weak for its burden, and knowest thou not that it suffers pains?'

But the man answered and said, 'What is that to you? I can beat it as much as I please, since it is my property, and I bought it for a good sum of money. Ask those that are with thee, for they know me, and know there-of.' And some of the disciples said, 'Yea Lord, it is as he says. We have seen how he bought it.' But the Lord said, 'Do you not notice how it bleeds, and do you not hear how it laments and cries?' But they answered and said, 'Nay Lord, we hear not how it laments and cries.' And the Lord was sad and exclaimed, 'Woe to you, that you hear not how it complains to the Creator in heaven, and cries for mercy. But three times woe to him of whom it complains and cries in its distress.' And he came forth and touched the animal. And it arose and its wounds were healed.

And Jesus said to the man, 'Now go on, and beat it no more, that you may also find mercy.'

This account, in an early Coptic manuscript, reminds not only the Christian, but all of us, that the animal inhabitants of the planet are also our neighbours. If we are in fact superior, as we maintain, then such superiority, far from giving us the right to abuse animals for selfish ends, whether in the name of science, medicine or food, in reality implies and requires of us an ethical duty of respect and care towards them, and the conscious recognition of the bond of compassion that should link us to all beings lower in the scale of evolution to us. If man is indeed the noble creature he claims to be, then *noblesse oblige*.

Ernest Scott, before quoting Burns, is referring to the communication that the Sufis Francis and his teacher Kubra are reputed to have had with animals, particularly birds, as we have mentioned earlier. He suggests that this kind of engagement has an evolutionary dimension, that the evolution, the real inner evolution of man and the animals, may be indissolubly linked, organically connected, at some deeper level not yet recognised—or perhaps forgotten.

And when we put hens in boxes, denying them all means of expression, depriving them of their natural God-given birthright to simply be themselves, in effect attempting to reduce their evolutionary level to the status of plants in pots—it is ultimately *ourselves* we are depriving and reducing.

It could be said that the message inherent in the story of Noah's Ark is that we are all in the same boat together. Not only did The Creator instruct Noah to give the animals passenger status in the Ark: but significantly He deemed them important enough to be included as parties to the contract He made after the Deluge.

And behold, I establish my covenant with you, and with your seed after you.

And with every living creature that is with you, of the fowl, of the cattle, and of every beast of the earth that is with you; from all that go out of the ark, to every beast of the earth. (Genesis 9.9–10)

The following account from *The Life of St Francis* by his contemporary and one-time pupil, Bonnaventura, is interesting:

As St. Francis went forth to preach he found a great quantity of birds gathered together, and when he saw them he ran to them and saluted them, and with great joy he beheld them. And it was great marvel, for there was not one of them that removed from their place, but all stood

St. Francis in the Marshes, by Paul Tricker

in peace and bowed their heads and stretched their necks, and attentively beheld him. When the holy man saw this he reasoned with them and urged them hear the word of God. Then he said to them in this wise, 'Fair brother and sister birds, you ought greatly to praise God who is your maker, who has clothed you from the rain with feathers, who has given you wings to fly with, and has granted you your living in the purity of the air without labour, who sustaineth and feedeth and governeth you.' When he had said many words to them the birds put out their necks and stretched their wings and opened their bills and beheld the man of God attentively, and with all their bodies made great joy after their fashion. And the holy man passed among them with great joy of spirit, and his coat touchcd them, and none of them moved from their place nor stirred their wings until he had given them his blessing and leave to depart from him. And when they had his blessing they all flew away.

And finally I would like to add the feelings expressed in this poem:

The Unforgetting

The goldfish in the bowl recalls the lake—
And in his fins fantastic fevers quake.

The parrot on the perch who chain'd clings
Remembers jungles wild with unprisoned wings

The guinea-pig confused by mindless men
Recalls the games he played within his den.

The rat that is abused by shapes in white
Yearns for the rustling grasses of the night.

Never do captive creatures e'er forget
The ancient natural freedoms they're bereft.

It is ironic to think that the humble guinea-pig was respected as a royal animal by the Incas in its native Andes. Is it not ethically incumbent on *us* to be willing to be the 'guinea-pigs' for our *own* diseases?

CHAPTER NINE

The miracles

If one accepts that there is a higher world, and that certain beings are capable of simultaneously inhabiting that realm and this, then it is possible to see that some of their actions, perhaps all, bestride and traverse both planes of existence. Such interventions probably occur more often than we realise. The supernormal usually disguises itself as the normal, the inexplicable as the explicable. But when such actions are made obvious, and thus dramatic, they are called 'miracles'.

Sufi teachers, however, including Jesus, employ miracles as teaching instruments, or teaching actions. They are an organic aspect of their whole teaching operation. They are not done to dazzle, but to develop. They are always designed to deliver a particular inner effect on the recipient or recipients, in an appropriate context. Their purpose is not marvel but travel.

It is reported of the Sufi Emir Hamza (died 1710) that he could 'slip into invisibility just by taking a sideways step, when his feet were at right angles to one another'. When asked about this or about other wonders he said: 'I forbid you to relate any wonder of mine without adding that the performance of wonders is for a purpose of self-improvement or passing power, not amazement or faith to others.'

Sufi teaching masters like Jesus perform the transdimensional actions called 'miracles' to communicate an inner developmental impact to the deeper self of a pupil or other witnesses which will vary according to the receiver's state. As such, miracles are in fact parabolic actions. Their purpose is transformative.

From this point of view the turning of water into wine by Jesus at Cana (John 2.1–10) is a miracle *about* miracles, telling us something of the essential nature of *all* his miracles: they are all about changing 'water' into 'wine'—the alchemical transformation, the refinement of consciousness, wine being a Sufi symbol for spiritual essence.[1] Thus, 'walking on water' is only superficially a demonstration of overcoming the laws of nature. Its primary significance is undoubtedly as a teaching action, an inner communication from master to pupils regarding their need to walk on their own waters, and capacity to still their own inner storms.

One can be sure, too, that in some way the 'feeding of the five thousand' (Matthew 15.32–39) represents not merely the miraculous distribution of ordinary food to the disciples and others present that day in the 'wilderness', but also the parallel transmission of spiritual sustenance. There is always more to the miracle than meets the eye.

In this connection it is interesting to hear about what Richard Drobutt, a member of the Nurbakhshi Order of Sufis, who has specialised in the study of Balkan, Caucasian and Turkish mystical methods, calls the 'Tincture Technique'. He says: 'The Sheikhs of the Suhrawardi Order of Sufis, as well as sundry Christian clerics of the Armenian and Coptic churches, follow this technique. Briefly, it is based on the belief that something taught to a sample group out of a whole community will improve that community as a whole, the teaching spreading telepathically from the 'treated' group to the rest. This is said to be a very ancient belief; according to the Romanian priest Epifaniu, the process, called by him 'dilution', is an essential part of the human learning-process. He adds that it was reputedly discovered and applied many thousands of years ago in

Babylon. All believers in this technique agree that it is reduced in efficiency by the mental activity of the attempt to pass on all teaching by speech or writing.'[2]

Speaking as a Westerner, Drobutt comments: 'It is generally speaking entirely strange to our set of thought to credit that knowledge can be passed on from one mind to another by a sort of *osmosis*. It is hard to visualise experience passing through the human community ... like moisture through earth, shall we say.'

Though the real operation of a teaching miracle is at a deeper level, it is likely that the element of wonder or astonishment involved is also there to play a role in the total event. The shock effect of the inexplicable, the utterly unexpected, may serve to open the receiver to the significant communication by disrupting his or her ordinary pattern of thought for a moment so that it can no longer act as a barrier to the reception of an inner transmission. Thus a miracle '*takes* one by surprise' to enable something inwardly important to happen. What this is, only the master knows.

This 'developmental' perspective on miracles is probably true also of what are called the 'healing miracles' of Jesus—without in the least denying their nature as acts of compassion in the obvious sense. Undoubtedly he did give sight to the blind, hearing to the deaf, and movement to the paralysed. But it is impossible not to be aware at the same time of a metaphorical meaning in such terms as 'blindness', 'deafness', and 'paralysis', and of the inner implications of the symbolism with which the narrative of these events is imbued. 'Arise, take up thy bed, and walk' must surely have an esoteric dimension relating to 'sleep' and 'awakening'. As also must Jesus's words to the man 'taken with palsy' at Capernaum: 'I say unto thee, Arise, and take up thy bed, and go thy way into thine *own house*.' (Mark 2.11)

Hopefully, enough has been said to illustrate the operational function of miracles in the teaching work of Jesus. He was not alone in this. All Sufi masters have used, and continue to use, miracles in the same way—as an intrinsic element in evolutionary education.

Miracles can of course occur without the presence, or rather the obvious presence, of the directing teacher. Nor are they themselves necessarily obvious. Many are unnoticed—the 'hidden miracles'. On the face of it the pattern of events seems not to have been disturbed. But something has happened. An 'impress' has been made. 'Miracles', Idries Shah tells us, 'exist to be recorded, inwardly, by a special organ of recognition.'

Notes

1. Thus Ibn el Farid, the great Sufi poet says: 'Our wine existed before the grape and the vine.'
2. See *New Research on Current Philosophical Systems*, Octagon Press, 1968, a valuable and unusual collection of first-hand reports from the field.

CHAPTER TEN

Jesus the individual

Whatever 'son of God' means, and it clearly means a special relationship,[1] a close and constant connection with the Almighty, it does not and can not mean, as some mystics suppose, such absorption in God that the individual self is extinguished. This curious notion—the result of a premature and overwhelming experience, wrongly interpreted—is the same kind of delusion as that of those gurus who wander wild-eyed through India proclaiming they are 'God'!

For, surely the most striking and obvious thing about the world around us is that it is a world of *individuals*—whether humans, animals, plants or even the very pebbles on the shore.

> As kingfishers catch fire, dragonflies draw flame;
> As tumbled over rim in roundy wells
> Stones ring; like each tucked string tells, each hung bell's
> Bow swung finds tongue to fling out broad its name;
> Each mortal thing does one thing and the same:
> Deals out that being indoors each one dwells;
> Selves—goes itself; *myself* it speaks and spells,
> Crying *What I do is me: for that I came.*

Nowhere has the intrinsic mystery of the self and its expression been celebrated so wonderfully as in that verse by the great poet Gerard Manley Hopkins.

While another poet, E. E. Cummings, simply puts it like this:

> Nothing is as something as one.

F. R. Leavis says: 'Only the individual is real', expressing the same insight into the nature of the Universe. Individuality indeed seems the very hallmark of God's creation. It would appear to be a special interest of His. Unsurprisingly for the Infinite Individual!

If I might add my own humble contribution to the theme:

> This is before all other versions
> Clearly a Universe of *persons*,
> Irreplaceably various,
> Often a bit precarious!
> Not (on the whole) divinities,
> But scintillating—
> With their own distinct infinities.

The suggestion is that we each have an intrinsic individual infinity within the greater Infinity of God, which is so extremely Supreme that only He can possibly understand it—and then perhaps He too only on a good day!

Sufism, therefore, is not a question of the human self effacing its own identity by some sort of absorbtion into the Infinite Self. It is rather, as Sirdar Iqbal Ali Shah affirms, 'the Infinite passing mysteriously into the human self, enhancing and vivifying it, making its identity more iridescent.' He continues 'The evolution of man consists in his gradual growth in self-possession, in uniqueness, and intensity.'

The business of the Sufis is the recovery and uncovering of man's inner self. As Hafiz puts it: 'You yourself are hidden under your own veil.' The aim is nothing less than that re-cognition of one's real nature from all that masquerades as it, expressed in the exhortation in which Jesus concurs with the Oracle at Delphi: 'Know Thyself'.

Jesus of Nazareth, whatever else he was or was not, impresses the reader of the Gospels most powerfully as an individual. He was God's man—but very much his *own* man too. In almost his every word, his every action, one senses the special tone, the distinct touch, the unique verve, of someone unmistakably and irreplaceably himself,[2] while honouring and cultivating the irreplaceability of others too—his Sufi task.

Oscar Wilde, whose greatness as a thinker has not yet been truly recognised by our culture, and whose wit has tended to obscure his wisdom, perceived Jesus as 'the supreme individualist'—and thus a man after his own heart! For Wilde believed that the cultivation of individuality was the very purpose of life. Reflecting in *De Profundis* on Jesus' teachings, he observes: 'It is tragic how few people ever "possess their souls" before they die.' Instead, he continues, 'they become possessed by other things …. What Jesus does say, is that man reaches his perfection, not through what he has, not even through what he does, but entirely through what he *is!*.'

And Wilde concludes: '"Know thyself!" was written over the portal of the ancient world. Over the portal of the new world "Be thyself" shall be written. And the message of Christ to man was simply "Be thyself". That is the secret of Christ.'

Of course, Jesus knew that these two aims are in fact one. Which, indeed, Oscar Wilde came to realise, too.

For only the person who is aware of the sacredness of his or her own individuality can truly respect the sacredness of other selves. How else can you "Love your neighbour as your self"?

If you don't love yourself you will find it difficult to love anyone else. Only the developed heart of the developed individual can perceive, can fully and deeply be aware of, can truly value, the especial beauty of other hearts. The development of consciousness increases one's sense of an inner bond with one's fellows. This is the real meaning of self respect. While selfishness on the other hand is a characteristic of the undeveloped heart.

It has been wisely said of the mystical ascent: 'The closer one comes to God, the closer one comes to oneself.' It is also true to say that the closer one comes to oneself, the closer one comes to God.

For the Sufis this involves a transformation of the personality, an intensification of the self, beyond the range of what is normally understood as mysticism. Nevertheless, it is relevant to hear of the experience of the Christian mystic, John Ruysbroeck in this matter: 'The naked spirit stands erect, it feels itself to be wrapped round, affirmed and affixed by the formless immensity of God, since our being, without losing anything of its personality, is united with the Divine Truth which respects all diversity.'

In the words of another mystic, Meister Eckhart: 'That we may be unique, and that our uniqueness may remain, God help us all!'

And helped we will be—if we allow ourselves to be, if we make ourselves *available* to help, by attuning ourselves to our truest need, with deepest discrimination.

For 'all that glitters is not gold'.

Conversely, all that is gold does not glitter.

The real spiritual entity may not seem 'spiritual'.

As Saadi has said: 'The touchstone it is which knows the real gold.'

And to uncover, to get in touch with that touchstone, there is no harm in a bit of humility, I understand!

I'd like to end with a poem:

The Call

Have you the ears to hear
The ancient roar
Of the Eternal breakers breaking
On time's shore?

And can you not remember
The unfading Fire behind the dying ember?

Seek you your real self lost upon the mountain?
And dare you face your face within the fountain?

Are you able
To find again and live your own true fable?

And can you not hear your own Completion call,
Beckoning,
From somewhere high above the Fall?

That is the only reckoning.

Notes

1. Called by al Qashani 'The essential relationship'. This, he says, 'is the relationship between Truth and the individual'. (*Istila-hat al—Sufiya*).
2. Blake sees this quality in Jesus and calls it the 'Poetic Genius'— the essential self he avers we are all capable of realising. It is interesting to note that originally to the Romans the 'genius' of a person meant his authentic nature, special to him or her, hence the word 'genuine'.

APPENDIX

The Hymn of the Pearl

Here is the great 'Hymn of the Pearl', sometimes called 'Hymn of the Soul', to be found in the Acts of Thomas in the New Testament Apocrypha, where it is attributed to the disciple Thomas during his teaching-journey in India.

When I was a child
in my Father's palace
in the East,
my parents decided
to send me down
to the land of
Egypt.

They gave me food
and other things
for a long sojourn,
and armed me with adamant.
They took off my golden robe,
and gave me ordinary clothes.
And they made a covenant with me,
a covenant they made,
inscribed on my heart
that I should not forget it.

'If thou go down into Egypt
and bring back
the one pearl
which is there
in the midst of the sea,
girt about by the serpent,
the loud-breathing serpent,
thou shalt again put on
thy golden garment,
thy royal robe
and become heir to us
in our kingdom.'

I came out of the East
by a difficult road,
with two guides given.
But when I entered Egypt
they left me,
and I was alone.

I set forth straightway to the serpent
and by his hole I abode,
watching
for him to slumber
that I might take my pearl
from him.

And I put on
the raiment of the Egyptians,
lest I should seem strange,
as one that had come from without
to recover the pearl;
and lest they should awake the serpent
against me.
But somehow they learned

I was not of their country,
and with guile they mingled for me
a deceit,
and I tasted of their food,
and I knew no more that I was a king's son,
and I became
a servant
unto their ruler.

And I forgot also the pearl,
for which my fathers had sent me,
and through the heaviness of their food
I fell
into a deep sleep.

But when this happened to me
my fathers became aware of it,
and grieved for me,
and decided to send me
this letter:
From thy Father the King of kings,
and thy mother that ruleth the East,
unto our son that is in Egypt, peace.
Rise up
and awake out of sleep
and hearken unto the words of the letter
and remember
that thou art a son of kings;
lo, thou hast come under the yoke of bondage.
Remember the pearl,
for which thou was sent
into Egypt.
Remember thy golden robe,
the glorious garment that thou shouldst wear.
Thy name is in the book of life,

and to us in our kingdom
thou must return.

The letter flew,
and down by me lighted,
and became all-speech.
And I at the voice of it
and the feeling of it
started up out of sleep,
and I took it up and kissed and read it.

And it was written concerning that
which was recorded in my heart,
and forthwith I remembered
I was a son of kings,
and my freedom yearned
after its kind.

I remembered the pearl
for which I was sent
down into Egypt.
I began with charms
against the terrible serpent,
and I overcame him
by naming the name of my Father upon him.
And I caught away the pearl
and turned
to bear it unto my fathers.

I stripped off the lowly garment
and left it in their land,
and directed my way forthwith
to the light of my fatherland
in the East.

And all the way
the letter flew before me
like a white bird fluttering,
with its light
guiding me back.

And from afar
I once again beheld my royal robe
which in a golden glow arose
to meet me,
and I entered its resplendence.

And then I was lifted up
into the place of peace,
and I bowed my head in homage
to my Father,
who had sent it to me.
For I had performed his commandments,
and he likewise
that which He had promised.

The King's Son

'The King's Son' is a Sufi teaching-story in traditional and current use—this version having been delivered by Amir Sultan, Sheikh of Bokhara, who taught in Istanbul. Juxtaposed with the foregoing text, it is hardly necessary to say that it testifies to the presence of an ongoing, living Tradition.

Once, in a country where all men were like kings, there lived a family, who were in every way content, and whose surroundings were such that the human tongue cannot describe them in terms of anything which is known to man today. This country of Sharq seemed satisfactory to the young prince Dhat, until one day his parents told him: 'Dearest son of ours, it is the necessary custom of our land for each royal prince, when he attains a certain age, to go forth on a trial. This is in order to fit himself for kingship and so that both in repute and in fact he should have achieved—by watchfulness and effort—a degree of manliness not to be attained in any other way. Thus it has been ordained from the beginning, and thus it will be until the end.'

Prince Dhat therefore prepared himself for his journey, and his family provided him with such sustenance as they could: a special food which would nourish him during an exile, but which was of small compass though of illimitable quantity.

They also gave him certain other resources, which it is not possible to mention, to guard him, if they were properly used.

He had to travel to a certain country, called Misr, and he had to go in disguise. He was therefore given guides for the journey, and clothes befitting his new condition: clothes which scarcely resembled one royal-born. His task was to bring back from Misr a certain Jewel, which was guarded by a fearsome monster.

When his guides departed, Dhat was alone, but before long he came across someone else who was on a similar mission, and together they were able to keep alive the memory of their sublime origins. But because of the air and food of the country, a kind of sleep soon descended upon the pair, and Dhat forgot his mission.

For years he lived in Misr, earning his keep and following a humble vocation, seemingly unaware of what he should be doing.

By a means which was familiar to them but unknown to other people, the inhabitants of Sharq came to know of the dire situation of Dhat, and they worked together in such a way as they could, to help to release him and to enable him to persevere with his mission. A message was sent by a strange means to the princeling, saying: 'Awake, for you are the son of a king, sent on a special undertaking, and to us you must return.'

This message awoke the prince, who found his way to the monster, and by the use of special sounds, caused it to fall into a sleep; and he seized the priceless gem which it had been guarding.

Now Dhat followed the sounds of the message which had woken him, changed his garb for that of his own land, and retraced his steps, guided by the Sound, to the country of Sharq.

In a surprisingly short time, Dhat again beheld his ancient robes, and the country of his fathers, and reached his home. This time, however, through his experiences, he was able to see that it was somewhere of a greater splendour than ever before, a safety to him; and he realised that it was the place commemorated vaguely by the people of Misr as Salamat: which they took to be the word for Submission, but which he now realised meant—peace.

POSTSCRIPT

Man's a mysterious creature—
He knows not who he is.
There's many a hidden feature
In the face he thinks is his.

One day he'll walk on water,
One day he'll talk to birds.
His feet no more will falter,
He'll speak unspoken words.

Out from the starry spaces
His kind shall call to him—
The other Human races,
And all the Seraphim.

FURTHER READING

The New Testament, Authorised Version (1611)
Despite overlay and interpolation still contains much original
core material, particularly Jesus's sayings and parables, which
remain intact. Superior to all modern translations because of
the English poet, William Tyndale's, inspired sensitivity to the
Nazarene poet's work.

The New Testament Apocrypha, M. R. James, Oxford University
Press
A diverse collection of extra-biblical writings of value if read
with discrimination. Contains 'The Hymn of the Pearl', within
the text entitled 'The Acts of Thomas'.

The Gospel of Thomas, Marvin Meyer (Translator)
Discovered in the sands of Egypt near Nag Hammadi in 1945,
this invaluable 2nd century document consists of a large number of parables and sayings of Jesus, known and unknown.
Confirms the existence of an essentially esoteric Christianity
for which it was clearly a working text.

The Mark, Maurice Nicoll, London, Vincent Stuart
Inner interpretation of the parables, occasionally too asser-
tive, but generally containing much original insight—in par-

ticular into the meaning of the Greek word *metanoia*, wrongly translated as 'repentance' but which actually means 'change of consciousness'—(*meta-nous*).

Among the Dervishes, O. M. Burke, London, Octagon Press
On a remarkable journey to the East and Middle East the traveller visits several ancient spiritual communities possessing unusual knowledge. Of particular interest is his encounter with a school of Christians near Herat in Afghanistan, claiming to have been directly founded by the master himself, and with a different understanding of his teachings. Corroborates at many points evidence presented by Holger Kersten in *Jesus Lived in India* (Element) that Jesus survived the crucifixion—to continue his work in Kashmir and Afghanistan.

The Mind Field, Robert Ornstein, Malor, ISHK, Massachusetts, Cambridge (UK distribution: Octagon Press)
A shrewd and witty guide, as lucid as it is acute, through what the author describes as the contemporary 'mindfield' of cults and pseudo-sufic entities. It contains a much-needed statement on the limitations of meditation, and generally assists in the somewhat important matter of distinguishing the path from the 'garden path'.

The Teachers of Gurdjieff, Rafael Lefort, London, Gollanz
A quest for the source of Gurdjieff's teaching. A journey which enriches both the author and the reader who accompanies him. Contains valuable material on the Christian-Sufi connection.

The People of the Secret, Ernest Scott, London, Octagon Press
The learned author develops with cumulative evidence his thesis of the influence upon human affairs of a 'Hidden Directorate', whose purpose is to guide the evolution of man, in harmony with a Cosmic Design.

Lost Bearings in Philosophy, Max Gorman, Corona
A short but concentrated monograph identifying and tracing the course of a wisdom-tradition from ancient Greek sages, through Alchemy, to the present day. Indicates the continuum between Romanticism and Mysticism, stressing the importance of intuition as a mode of intelligence.

Tales of the Dervishes, Idries Shah, London, Octagon Press
A collection of Sufi teaching stories in current use, selected from the classics, from oral tradition, and from unpublished manuscripts. It contains several tales of early Christian origin.

A Perfumed Scorpion, Idries Shah, London, Octagon Press
An invaluable introduction to present day Sufi activity, based on a series of lectures. As entertaining as it is educational.

INDEX

9 781911 597087